France and her army

Charles de Gaulle

Nabu Public Domain Reprints:

You are holding a reproduction of an original work published before 1923 that is in the public domain in the United States of America, and possibly other countries. You may freely copy and distribute this work as no entity (individual or corporate) has a copyright on the body of the work. This book may contain prior copyright references, and library stamps (as most of these works were scanned from library copies). These have been scanned and retained as part of the historical artifact.

This book may have occasional imperfections such as missing or blurred pages, poor pictures, errant marks, etc. that were either part of the original artifact, or were introduced by the scanning process. We believe this work is culturally important, and despite the imperfections, have elected to bring it back into print as part of our continuing commitment to the preservation of printed works worldwide. We appreciate your understanding of the imperfections in the preservation process, and hope you enjoy this valuable book.

FRANCE AND HER ARMY

FRANCE AND HER ARMY

by
CHARLES DE GAULLE

Translated by
F. L. DASH

HUTCHINSON & CO. (Publishers), LTD.
LONDON :: NEW YORK :: MELBOURNE :: SYDNEY

THIS BOOK IS PRODUCED IN
COMPLETE CONFORMITY WITH THE
AUTHORISED ECONOMY STANDARDS.

PRINTED IN
GREAT BRITAIN,
AT THE ANCHOR
PRESS, TIPTREE,
::   ESSEX   ::

CONTENTS

	PAGE
ORIGINS	7
ANCIEN RÉGIME	23
THE REVOLUTION	33
NAPOLEON	45
FROM DISASTER TO DISASTER	61
BETWEEN TWO WARS	75
THE GREAT WAR	90

"*Mère, voyez vos fils, qui se sont tant battus!*"
—Péguy.

ORIGINS

I

[FRANCE WAS FASHIONED BY THE SWORD. OUR FOREFATHERS MADE THEIR ENTRY on to the stage of history with the sword of Brennus. Roman arms brought them civilization. After the fall of the Empire the country regained consciousness of itself, thanks to the axe of Clovis. The *fleur-de-lys*, the symbol of national unity, owes its origin to the three-pronged javelin.]

But although a state may be created by force of arms, yet the waging of war is of no avail save as an instrument of policy. So long as the country was covered by the dense forest of Feudalism, blood flowed in vain on to the barren soil. From the day which marked the union of a strong government and a powerful army, France became a nation.

[The fury of the Gauls had been broken by the military art of the Legions.] By throwing down his arms at Caesar's feet Vercingetorix did no more, it is true, than invest the loss of independence with a tragic shroud of glory. Perhaps, too, by this desperate act of submission to discipline, he wished to teach his race an imperishable lesson. The victor, in any case, undertook the task of educating the vanquished foe, and for five hundred years Rome was to impress upon our laws and customs, our language, our monuments, our roads and our artistic creations the stamp of her order and authority, while manifesting to a score of generations the spirit of military might. From that experience sprang the idea —or the nostalgic desire—of a centralized state and a regular army, an ideal which survived all the vicissitudes of the Barbarian invasions.

For several centuries, however, the Roman order suffered an eclipse. The Merovingians made some attempt to utilize the remaining fragments of Roman organization. On the Catalaunian Fields Clodion mingled his hordes with the cohorts of Aëtius. Clovis, as Gallo-Roman consul, created a well-knit force. As Duke of the French, Charles Martel led good troops against the Saracens at Poitiers, while the Carolingians attempted to restore both the Empire and the army. Charlemagne imposed upon his subjects compulsory military service, and led well-trained legions of conscripts as far as the Tiber, the Ebro, the Oder, and the Danube. But all these last strivings towards order were finally wrecked by the superior force of centrifugal tendencies. [In the chaos of races, passions, and interests, the central authority became a fiction, and military art a remembrance. As security, however, must have the support of some kind of authority, Feudalism imposed its rule as an antidote to anarchy.]

By splitting up sovereignty into as many fragments as there were claimants, who, by violence or cunning, could grab a share of it, the feudal system multiplied frontiers *ad infinitum*. A host of local disputes, which would formerly have been settled by law, could no longer find any solution except by force of arms. A long series of struggles began between one fief and another on the subject of dues, inheritances, and boundaries—disputes concerning details which no longer aroused any widespread popular feeling. [The feudal principle was a kind of bargain whereby the benefits received from the overlord were paid for in service. The fortunes of the vassals depended on those of the lord. As for the humble peasants, they were linked by a multitude of bonds to their local chief, who provided them with house and field, administered justice, and lived among them.] A man's obligation to follow his master to war was, however, subject to conditions varying widely according to time and place. The effect, as far as military forces were concerned, was great diversity in composition. Before undertaking any expedition the suzerain was obliged to negotiate for the co-operation of his vassals.

The latter presented themselves with their arms at the appointed time and place. They were assembled by their feudal lords on the "Champ de Mai", where lords and lordlings, accompanied by their own retainers, contingents provided by the towns, the corporations and the monasteries, were joined by adventurers prepared to risk their lives in return for food. Each group, roughly gathered round its own standard, was known and scrutinized by all the others. While the leaders prepared to assert their rival claims, the crowds of humble folk extolled the valour of their own cantons with shouts of "Beauvais! Beauvais!" "Châtillon!" or "Long live Coucy!" Meanwhile the troop marshals appointed by the suzerain endeavoured to calm the tumult, form bodies of horse or foot, assemble the mechanics to work the machines, and reduce the crowd of camp-followers and the baggage to some semblance of order.

The fractions which constituted the army had no more homogeneity than the army itself. Here and there one of the nobles might appear at the head of a numerous escort, or a township would draw up an orderly line of soldiers. But a vassal of noble birth brought nothing but his own person, while certain groups were no more than a useless rabble. Even so, each man agreed to serve only within stipulated limits. There were, presumably, few knights who showed themselves as intransigent as a certain Guillaume de la Roche, who claimed that he owed the king no more than one day's service a year, and that only in the district of Tonnay-Boutonne; but all were able to produce contracts which limited their period of service, promises that they would not have to go outside a certain region, assurances that they would not march if others did not do so. There were prescriptive rights concerning routes, quarters, and battle order. The desire for privilege and the love of equality—those dominating and contradictory passions of Frenchmen of every age—found ample material for endless discussions.

Since a knight imposed his rights upon the mass of his humble followers by force, and was unable in return to count with certainty upon the support of his reluctant vassals, he had to arm himself so as to be able to ward off every attack by his own resources. Hence he was armoured in front, behind, and on the sides. He was padded with leather and steel plates from his neck to his feet, and bore a heavy helmet on his head and a stout shield on his arm. In course of time the blacksmith's art was to replace the clumsy carapace by jointed armour. Our knight wielded the mace, the flail, the battle-axe, the lance riveted to his side, and the enormous two-handed sword. Thus equipped he was borne by a sturdy horse, protected like its rider by armour, so that horseman and mount might be compared with some massive castle-keep.

It is true that the army included other elements besides this mobile fortress. The knights needed helpers. Every knight had his henchmen who carried and polished his weapons, looked after his baggage, groomed his horses, led him into battle (since he was virtually blind and deaf under his helmet), hoisted him into the saddle, and ran to his assistance when he was unhorsed. The team of assistants comprised anything from a solitary servant to a numerous staff of squires and arms-bearers constituting, with the knight himself, the tactical unit of feudal troops, the "lance", that is, a knight surrounded by his retainers.

Although the infantry, in the strict sense of the term, was relegated to the background, it had not altogether disappeared. The feudal lord took care to recruit serfs from his own domains, while, in addition, numerous towns, communes, and corporations were obliged to provide contingents of foot-soldiers. At the beginning of each campaign, therefore, troops of infantry assembled, armed with bows, spears, pikes, sometimes with scythes, slings and pointed stakes, and more or less protected with coats of mail, quilted coats, and bucklers. It is a far cry from this heterogeneous infantry to the ancient phalanxes and legions. Deficient in zeal, in training and in armament, the soldiery was anything but reliable. Certain districts, however, such as Flanders, Switzerland,

Gascony, where the old civic spirit had retained its vitality, provided a trustworthy militia. Many towns, moreover, rather than mobilize their burgesses, preferred to furnish their suzerain with professional soldiers. These trained bands, under vigorous leadership, showed (when they had a mind to it) considerable courage and resource.

When we consider the way in which these armies were recruited, it is easy to understand that discipline was of the most rudimentary kind. The leader, were he king or prince, enjoyed but a precarious authority. William the Conqueror took ten years to raise the forces he required to enforce his claim to the duchy of Normandy. During the First Crusade, after Nicaea, Antioch, and Arca, the combined authority of the leaders could not prevent the Christian army from melting away like snow in the sun. Tradition has it that before the battle of Bouvines Philip Augustus gathered his barons around him and, while food and drink were being prepared for them, took the precaution of pleading with any who might be meditating trickery or knavery.

It is true that the "point of honour" compensated to some extent for the insubordination of feudal armies. In the eyes of this warlike society, not far removed from the days when a prince was merely a warrior raised upon the shield, a duke a military leader, and a count a companion in arms, a man's reputation, his titles and fortune, were acquired by combat. The education of young men of noble birth aimed, therefore, at developing their valour and their warlike vigour. From the age of seven, as pages, squires and, finally, as knights, they were trained physically for war and morally for deeds of daring. Moreover, in spite of hunting, jousting, feasting, and despite the charms of languishing and neglected châtelaines, the existence of a youth in a gloomy mediaeval castle was melancholy enough to make him dream of adventure. As for men of lesser rank, their only hope of ennoblement lay in their prowess as soldiers. A villein, singled out by his lord, might become a squire. Thereafter, his good services might be rewarded by a fief. From this it resulted that the principal combatants on the battlefield showed the greatest zeal in order to distinguish themselves. Thus the audacity and skill of the individual, though badly combined and often rash or even absurd, endowed the military operations of the time with a character of heroism which offset their lack of coherence.

In point of fact the struggles between feudal lords were not usually characterized by any great determination. Each side endeavoured to damage the other by raids and skirmishes, avoiding pitched battles as far as possible. Not that caution was always carried so far as to "wage the campaign for five years without meeting once", as in the war narrated by Girard de Roussillon. Even when battle was joined the two armies were not completely engaged, each side leaving the task of settling the quarrel to a few champions. Hostilities were constantly suspended by a "Truce of God" or a "king's quarantine", and from the autumn to the spring the warriors stayed at home. If things were going badly, moreover, there was always the expedient of shutting oneself up in one's castle or fortified town. There, behind walls of tremendous thickness, one could safely wait for better days. To lay a regular siege to a fortified place, with battering-rams, catapults and mines placed beneath the ramparts, or to storm it with scaling-ladders or wooden towers built up to battlement height, demanded a degree of method and perseverance in the attacker which was rarely to be found. Sometimes, however, passions reached boiling-point and war was waged in deadly earnest. But Simon de Montfort lost twenty thousand men in taking Béziers and Carcassonne from the Albigensians; Philip I "grew old" in destroying Montléry; while it took Louis VI three years to reduce the keep of Puiset Castle.

At certain moments of dire peril France became conscious of her national identity. When the people of Paris were defending the passage of the Seine against the Normans under Rollo, the whole country prayed for their success. The invasion of French soil by the Emperor Otto in alliance with the Count of

Flanders gave rise to a real movement of popular resistance to the invaders. At other times the mass of the population was at one with the aristocracy in their enthusiasm for conquest. The invasion of England by William the Conqueror, the foundation of the Norman-French kingdom of the Two Sicilies, and the establishment of a son of the Duke of Burgundy on the throne of Portugal all attracted large numbers of plebeian volunteers. Almost a million villeins set out on the First Crusade in the company of sixty thousand knights. These wars of national defence, conquest or proselytism assumed an entirely different character from that of the usual military escapades. Poitiers, Hastings, Bouvines, Dorylaion, Mons-en-Puelle were great battles in which the little men fought with as much determination as their lords.

Nevertheless, in these vast conflicts as in local squabbles, the efforts of a medley of troops, commanded by leaders unskilled in the art of war and insecure in their authority, were made amidst the utmost confusion. The dispositions of the army, the time and place of the action, were decided by custom and convention. Nothing would have persuaded the Crusaders of Bouillon to go into action under the command of the Count of Toulouse. At Bouvines the burgesses of Soissons, in their capacity as privileged vassals of the Abbot of Saint-Médard, would never have given way to the peasant militia of Péronne. It needed the discovery, in a church in Antioch, of the spear which pierced the side of Christ to persuade the Christian army to march against the Emir Kerboga. There was, of course, no system of, and often no provision for, supplies, quarters or medical care, with the result that an army's progress was marked by pilfering and waste, while the fighting-men were surrounded by a noisy swarm of merchants, labourers and beggars. Famine and epidemics inevitably followed. At the siege of Antioch the poor wretches in the bands of Tafur were reduced to eating human corpses. At Hattin, owing to the lack of arrangements for a supply of water, the Crusaders were driven mad by thirst. At Damietta and, later, at Tunis a dreadful epidemic of dysentery put an end to the crusade of Louis IX.

In such conditions the armies of the day could perform only the most rudimentary concerted movements. Once the enemy was sighted, if an engagement was desired, the army marched straight towards him. First came the vanguard of well-tried men. There followed the armed mob divided up into its component parts, advancing along the road with scant attention to any marching order. As the danger approached the excitement increased, expressing itself in oaths, challenges, and prayers which were intended to encourage the disorderly crowd. However, since they were now in full view of the enemy, something had to be done about marshalling all these fragments into their battle order. This task fell to the leaders' "companions" and took hours to perform—provided, that is, that the prevailing chaos allowed the operation to be completed at all. While this was going on the leaders held a council of war. Somehow or other decisions were taken and the rôles assigned. Then the battle began.

The action was usually opened by the infantry. Bowmen, preceding the main body, which advanced in loose formation, exchanged arrows with the enemy, while ready to dart back to shelter behind the more heavily armed infantry. Sometimes a particularly bold battalion would surge forward in serried ranks and assail the enemy with mighty thrusts and blows of pike and sword. This was what the mercenaries of Guillaume des Barres did at Courtray and, later, the Flemish infantry at Bruges, and the German mercenaries at Bouvines. But everybody realized that this was only a prelude to the real battle, namely, the engagement of the chivalry.

The knights are drawn up and await their turn. Each knight has put on his helm and breastplate, has seized his weapons and taken up his position. On his left side, where he finds it difficult to strike, he has placed his carefully chosen seconds. The squires hold aloft the banners so that the vassals can recognize their own suzerain. The signal is given and the line advances with cries of "Out! Out!" from each warrior beneath his armour. This is no dashing onslaught, for the chargers, with a weight of four hundred pounds on their backs, cannot sustain a gallop for long. In a cloud of dust and with a clatter of iron, all lances couched, the wall of armour reaches the enemy. The infantry are of course incapable of standing up to the charge. To do so would require a coolness and a skill in opening and closing their ranks which they are far from possessing. The first result of the engagement of the cavalry is therefore, in most cases, the flight of the foot-soldiers. This, quite apart from any question of flattery or boasting, explains the heroic exploits recounted in the epic poems of the time. The scattered infantry keeps well out of the way until its own cavalry has attacked in its turn. When it does so there is a deafening *mêlée* between the opposing masses of chivalry.

This duel is a severe test of endurance. To cut and thrust and parry needs great muscular effort beneath a suit of armour. But all this rough-and-tumble, all these attacks with the point of the lance or the edge of the sword, cause very little bloodshed. There are much-dented armour, many bruised limbs and broken lances, and very few dead. A chronicler who fought at Brenneville wrote: "There are two hundred lords engaged in this battle; few were slain, for they were covered in iron and strove rather to take one another that they might hold each other to ransom than to kill one another." Big losses among the knights occurred only as a result of some trap or unexpected disaster. They were crushed beneath the boulders of Roncevaux; many perished of thirst at Hattin; others were drowned in the canal at Courtray. In any case the great lords were the main target. If they could be taken prisoner, they would pay a bigger ransom for their liberty; while if they were killed, their vassals would lose their main incentive to fight. The battle, therefore, was fought in separate groups round the most important leaders—round the king if he were present. Louis VI, seized by some English soldiers at Brenneville, was released only with great difficulty. At Laodicaea Louis VII had to fight alone for some time amidst a crowd of Saracens; while at Bouvines, Philip Augustus, unhorsed by the German foot-soldiers, was in great danger of being killed or captured.

The intensive stage of the struggle, however, entailing so much muscular effort and nervous strain, was of short duration. The combatants soon reached the point of exhaustion; and it was then that the early advantage of one side in numbers, position or speed, made itself felt, for it was almost impossible to retrieve an unfavourable situation by attacking with such unwieldy, slow-moving material. Once the line was broken, therefore, there was little likelihood of closing it again, despite the exploits of the bravest, who found themselves gradually deserted by the others. It was at this point that the foot-soldiers on the winning side would return to the rescue. It was no part of their job to attack unscathed knights in armour, but to slink up behind those who appeared to be in a bad way, to bring them down by ham-stringing their horses, and then to deal with the poor wretches as they lay unarmed and powerless.

In such a case the hard-pressed army would be able to fight back only by a supreme effort of discipline. But self-sacrifice in adversity is something that only well-trained bodies of troops can show. In feudal armies there were plenty of men who were brave, or even rash, so long as hope remained unshaken. But when the moment came for individuals to sacrifice themselves for their cause, personal considerations gained the upper hand. In most cases, therefore, the resistance of the losing side collapsed suddenly. The chivalry scattered like sheep, so that even the troubadours were hard put to it to explain their headlong flight. The infantry, alone and helpless, was hacked to pieces, while the commanders, abandoned by their companions, sought safety in some refuge. Distracted fugitives poured into the nearest friendly keeps or into those fortified towns which consented to open their gates. The pursuit did not last long, however, for the most determined victor was apt to lose his ardour for the chase when there was so much booty to be collected, so many estates, castles, and towns to be plundered.

It will be seen that the art of combination in warfare, which had been brought to such a pitch of perfection by certain peoples of antiquity, reached its decline in the customs and institutions of feudalism. It was not a question of defective material, either in quantity or quality. The *élite* possessed an individual skill in the use of weapons and a spirit in attack which have never been surpassed; the masses were docile and cheap; their leaders, having assumed command by right of birth at an age when their vigour was unimpaired, were men experienced in war and ready to take personal risks. But the cohesion which can be attained only by troops who are subjected to a uniform discipline and are accustomed to live, suffer, and act in common, was lacking in feudal warfare. The feudal army represented a chance grouping of unrelated fractions, rather than the closely bound assemblage of complementary parts which is a prerequisite of success in every sphere of human action.

Yet the valour of these feudal warriors did not fail to bear fruits which brought glory, if not always profit, to their country. Islam was halted on the frontiers of Aquitaine; Britain was conquered by men from the other side of the Channel who were to provide the aristocracy which became the backbone of England's might; the Germanic tribes were kept in check; dynasties of French blood were established in Naples and Portugal; French kingdoms were founded in Asia, and an empire in Greece, by campaigns whose renown has not perished after the lapse of eight centuries. In order to measure the tireless audacity of our feudal ancestors one has only to see, still standing on the hills of Lebanon, the fortresses which they built and defended for a century and more in an untamed country and an exhausting climate. Nor did the warlike ardour of the Middle Ages fail to produce certain beneficial effects of a moral order. It is not a matter of indifference that an epoch exalted courage and honour above all else. It is good that the spirit of chivalry, like some beautiful flower growing on the thorny stem of battle, should have succeeded in ennobling, though not in mitigating, the horrors of war.

II

Meanwhile, amidst all the storm and stress, the kings worked for unity. Merovingians, Carolingians, and Capetians all tended the flame of national feeling which was already bright in the days of the Gauls and continued to burn on the ruins of the Empire. Each king in his turn strove to bring into one whole the territories which had been dispersed for so long by exchange or conquest, as dowries or legacies. For although feudalism involved a perpetual dispersal, it could also be used to recover and unite. When the king of France confiscated, purchased, married or enfranchised, he did so by right of his suzerainty. In the thirteenth century the process seems to be almost complete: Louis IX, Philip the Bold, and Philip the Fair reigned in theory and in fact over the greater part of the former territory of Gaul. Later, Philip VI was the unchallenged ruler of three-quarters of the kingdom, suzerain in respect of their French fiefs of the kings of England, Navarre, and Majorca, an ally of the kings of Bohemia and Scotland, a relative of the rulers of Naples and Hungary, and the protector of the Pope at Avignon.

However, the feudal system began to show signs of decadence. The best of the nobles had perished in the Crusades. The others had returned from the East with luxurious tastes, ruinous alike to their purse and their reputation. Most important of all, the absence of the lord from his fief had resulted in a weakening of loyalty. Vassals had become disaffected; rights had lapsed and reverted to the suzerain. Many of the gentry who had hitherto been intimately connected with local affairs found themselves uprooted, with the result that dues appeared heavier than ever. The country districts heard the first low rumblings of discontent which were to culminate in the Jacquerie and the revolts of the Maillotins, Cabochians and others. At the same time new forces appeared before the public eye; towns gained their enfranchisement, monasteries received safeguards, and corporations acquired privileges. New industries—cotton, glass, mirrors, silk, paper—and new enterprises—the building of churches, markets, and roads—brought wealth to intelligent burgesses. The first universities, in Paris, Angers, Orleans, Toulouse, Montpellier, were demonstrating the superior power of the mind over matter. In many parts of the country "Parliaments" were soon to substitute the king's justice for that of the lords. The taste for communal undertakings was everywhere gaining the upper hand over the habit of personal enterprises. The thirteenth century built as many cathedrals as castles. The aristocracy was itself losing its youthful spirit whence it had drawn its strength and its grace. What must have been the corruption which made the twenty-year-old Margaret of Scotland exclaim before her death: "A fig for life! Speak to me of it no more!"

Developments of this kind were bound to have repercussions in the military field. Armed force had hitherto been the monopoly of the feudal lords. Their decline was accompanied by a weakening of the military system which depended exclusively on them. This was even more marked because this innovating age transformed weapons no less than customs. Despite the ban of the Lateran Council, the crossbow, which had been introduced from Asia, was already in widespread use and was making it possible for well-trained foot-soldiers to stand up to the chivalry. It was no longer a case of a wooden bow shooting wooden arrows which failed to pierce metal, but of hard armour-piercing iron bolts, hurled by a mechanically tightened steel bow and guided along a groove. And the dawn of the fourteenth century saw the appearance of cannon. It is true that these early bombards, cast-iron tubes stuffed with fragments of iron, possessed no great range or accuracy. But such as they were they thundered and belched fire, scaring the horses and even killing man and beast. Before long, loaded with cannon-balls, they were capable of blowing a hole in the walls of a castle-keep.

The decline of feudalism should have led the kings of France to create an armed force capable of waging war under the new conditions. A standing army had become a necessity. This need had been felt more or less clearly by royal governments for some time. Louis VI, on the advice of Suger, had tried to organize the militia of certain communes; Philip Augustus endeavoured to transform bands of mercenaries into well-disciplined troops; Louis IX had formed a corps of crossbowmen and another of engineers, each having its commander, its pay, and even a system whereby old soldiers could be pensioned off as lay monks of a monastery or as inmates of the Quinze-Vingts Hospital in Paris. But these unco-ordinated measures did not constitute a reorganization of the system. Failure to carry out the necessary reforms in time was to bring disaster on the monarchy.

When Edward III disembarked at Saint-Vaast-la-Hougue in July 1346 he brought with him a very different army from any that had hitherto been seen in France. His thirty-two thousand men were organized, armed and trained, with the result that the French were surprised and overwhelmed at the outset. The English archers, drawn up in regular companies, were skilful bowmen, trained to make the best use of the ground and to erect stockades. The horsemen were well-ordered and manœuvrable. Finally, use was made of bombards which were placed among the infantry. The first French bands to come up against these fine troops were the militia of Caen. "As soon as the burgesses saw the English advancing in three battles," says Froissart, "in close and powerful array, perceived their pennons and heard the road of those archers which they were not wont to see, they were so dismayed that no man in the world could have stayed them from flight." Throughout the whole course of the Hundred Years' War the enemy was to be the master of the battlefield. It is true that France, twice on the point of collapse, nevertheless recovered. Small engagements carried out by a few scattered bands, the resistance offered by towns and castles, the ingenuity and determination of certain leaders, and above all, the growing national feeling, created increasing difficulties for the English who, in the end, succumbed to them. But Crécy, Poitiers, and, later, Agincourt saw the beginning of a period in which neither numbers nor daring were of any avail when matched against art, discipline, and armament.

It was not that feudal France lacked the means for resisting her enemies. To give battle to the eighteen thousand English troops entrenched near Crécy, fifteen thousand Genoese bowmen, twenty thousand irregulars and several corps of militia were hastily recruited. In addition there were ten thousand knights, among whom were some of the most powerful lords. But this host was unorganized. When it moved off under the orders of Philip VI it had to march six leagues in the pouring rain, a circumstance which was sufficient to destroy any semblance of order: "Neither the king nor the marshals were masters of their men." It would have been prudent to delay the opening of hostilities until the following day, especially as the Genoese archers, "cruelly tired and worn out with marching more than six leagues fully armed", seeing that the strings of their crossbows were drenched and useless, begged their officers to let them get their breath and dry themselves. But the headstrong lords forced the king to give the order: "Let our Genoese advance and begin the battle!"

The crossbowmen retreated beneath the shower of arrows and shot against which they could do nothing, whereupon the lords, furious to see "these rascals encumbering the ground", charged in among them, their exhausted horses slipping on the wet ground. The arms of the English bowmen, the hail of shot from the bombards, created chaos among the attackers until, finally, the knights, overthrown by the Black Prince's men-at-arms, who had been kept under cover and in formation until they launched their attack, were completely routed. Such were the successive phases of this defeat which, in two hours, laid France open to the invader.

Ten years later, at Poitiers, the feudal army showed no more wisdom. The Black Prince was entrenched on a hill covered with vineyards and hedges. The only access to his position was by a steep path. The French vanguard, consisting of the flower of the chivalry, made a headlong charge, piled up until it could advance no further, until, under the blows of the enemy, these rash assailants were driven back on to the main body behind them. Panic seized half the army, which fled without having fought. The others stayed with John the Good, but in a state of great confusion. To make things worse, the French knights had sent back their horses, fearing that they would be terrified, as at Crécy, by the bombards. When the English charged in their turn, the knights fought back on foot, paralysed by their armour, to be overcome at last by the men-at-arms of the Prince of Wales. Despite prodigies of valour King John himself was made prisoner.

Thus, as a result of the failure to adapt her arms to the new conditions, France was plunged into the worst crisis of her history. As a consequence of the King's captivity and the military collapse, there followed not only invasion but a spate of treachery and disorder amidst which the nation was within an ace of total destruction. The Dauphin, who later became Charles V, had to organize resistance while the States-General fomented revolution. Etienne Marcel stirred up revolt in Paris, murdering the ministers. Charles the Bad carried on a civil war of his own, while the members of the Jacquerie were hanging the lords and burning down their châteaux.

In such conditions no military reforms were possible. After Poitiers, it is true, at the insistence of the States-General, the "Great Ordinance" of 1357 was promulgated, by virtue of which "every man in France shall be armed"—a vain proclamation by politicians, which raised no troops. In fact during a long period, all idea of engaging in pitched battles was abandoned. Local resistance and attacks by partisans were the means by which the English and the renegades who supported them were finally overcome, not without multiplying the horrors of war to the point of devastating the whole country. In return for many an enfranchisement or promise by the king, numerous towns undertook to build ramparts to be manned by the militia when the enemy appeared. Desperadoes like Duguesclin, Clisson, Renty, Boucicaut and Arnaud de Cervole roamed the country at the head of bands of mercenaries. These, in the fourteenth century, were easily raised, for anarchy in Italy, poverty in Germany, the war against the Infidels in Spain, Hungary and the Balkans, produced swarms of beggars and adventurers in every corner of Europe.

In this way the English, weary and bewildered, and, what is more, widely scattered as a result of their taste for good living and the necessities of the occupation, were gradually expelled from French territory. But what a price had to be paid for a military system of this kind! Almost the whole of the king's resources was absorbed by the mercenaries, who in addition extorted innumerable taxes from the population, taking provisions and quarters, plundering public money and treasure, selling safe-conducts and rights of way. What is more, this guerilla warfare provoked dreadful reprisals. Both sides competed in massacring, plundering, and burning, so that whole provinces were literally emptied of men and property. All this at the expense of the innocent inhabitants. When, at last, the national peril had passed, the king's government had no more urgent task than to rid the country of these powerful armed bands.

But even these terrible lessons proved useless in teaching our leaders common sense. Scarcely had Charles V died when France was once more torn by fierce dissensions. Charles VI was a child, who, when he reached manhood, was to become insane. The factions exploited the situation to resume their civil strife. The crimes of the royal princes, treachery on the very steps of the throne, the death-struggle between the Burgundians and the Armagnacs, risings in Paris and the Jacquerie in the country districts—all combined to give the English the opportunity to attempt another invasion. In 1415 Henry V landed near Harfleur with twenty-four thousand bowmen, six thousand mounted men-at-arms, and bombards—a small but well-trained army on the model of those of Edward III and the Black Prince. Once again France, prevented by internal strife and general apathy from creating a standing army, could confront the enemy only with the rabble of an outworn feudalism.

At Agincourt ten thousand French foot-soldiers met the fifteen thousand men which remained to the English after their costly capture of Harfleur. The battle was fought on a plain of ploughland, soaked by rain and hemmed in between woods into which the heavy cavalry was careful not to penetrate, but which the enemy had manned with archers. Realizing the restricted area of the ground the Constable d'Albret wished to dispose the three bodies of his army in depth. But every one of the leaders insisted on being in the front, with the result that there was hopeless congestion. Moreover, the knights, terrified of the cannon and crossbows, had increased the weight of their armour to such a degree that they were scarcely able to wield their lances and swords. In the words of Lefebre de Saint-Rémy, "they were borne down with exceeding long and heavy steel coats, in addition to their harness and their headpieces". As for the archers and the bombards, they were kept so far to the rear that they could not be used.

Although the foremost troops were paralysed by their very numbers, both flanks did succeed in making some headway. But as they skirted the edges of the woods they were attacked from the side and from behind by the English bowmen and sustained serious losses. In great disorder they reached the enemy line, which repelled them without difficulty. As they retreated they became entangled with the main body of their own troops. This was the signal for the English infantry to press home the attack in the centre and on both flanks. The French army was no longer anything but a chaotic struggling mass of men and horses, in which the great sword-blows of the professional soldiers bred panic, developing into a disorderly flight. Seven thousand were killed, three thousand taken prisoner, while the English losses amounted to less than six hundred men.

The defeat of Agincourt meant the literal disintegration of France. The dukes of Brittany, Anjou, and Burgundy signed treaties of neutrality with the English. The Paris mob massacred thousands of Armagnacs in their prisons. At Troyes, Isabelle of Bavaria recognized by treaty Henry V's claim to the throne; and on his death, three years later, his son Henry VI was proclaimed king of France, and recognized as such by the capital, the *Parlement*, the University, and by nearly the whole of the country north of the Loire which Bedford governed in the name of the English king. Meanwhile at Bourges, the young Charles VII, with neither an army nor money, surrounded by all the intrigues and quarrels which accompany misfortune, kept alight the feeble flame of French hopes.

Once again the national recovery was to depend on makeshift measures. Orleans, the only town remaining in the king's hands, was defended by no more than five hundred partisans and by its burgesses. At Patay the French army consisted at most of five thousand men from all sources. The attack on Rouen in 1432 was carried out by a handful of adventurers, anxious above all for booty. The leaders, Xaintrailles, Dunois, la Hire, Boussac, concerned themselves, therefore, with small-scale engagements, a procedure which prolonged the war and added to its devastation, but which at least did afford the country the opportunity of pulling itself together. The most remarkable feature of the epic of Joan of Arc was that the blows then struck had the support and the approval of the population. At Orleans, Jargeau and Beaugency, it was the attitude of the people, whose new and unexpected enthusiasm surprised and demoralized the English, that contributed to the defeat of the enemy. Henceforward the invaders could put up no more than a sullen defence. The coronation of the king at Rheims had the result of extending enormously the country's resurgent patriotism. When Paris was attacked, the presence of Joan before the Saint-Honoré gate aroused such intense enthusiasm among the townspeople that this alone was almost enough to procure her entry into the capital. Richemont skilfully exploited the psychological impulse. Shortly afterwards the Duke of Burgundy was to renounce the hateful alliance and to come over to the national cause. Paris opened its gates to the king, and the English, divided within by the Wars of the Roses, and deprived of reinforcements—for the bowmen were no longer willing to sign on for a campaign which had become unpopular—were pressed back yard by yard to the sea.

This time the dearly bought experience was not lost. In 1439, with the consent of the States-General, Charles VII promulgated the Orleans Ordinance which created a standing army. Henceforth the king would have at his disposition a force consisting of fifteen "companies of gendarmerie", each of one hundred "lances", or units, of six men, that is, a total of nine thousand horsemen.

As for the foot-soldiers and mechanics, the improvised formations of the feudal period were replaced, in part, by paid companies of crossbowmen and *bideaux*, and by artillery units or cannoneers. Henceforward, the fitful heroism of the paladins, the cunning of partisans and the short-lived zeal of the militia were replaced by the steady devotion of professional soldiers who, for three centuries and a half, were to be the bastion of France.

III

⟨It needed more than an ordinance to transform the army into a regular and permanent military body.⟩ There was a long period of transition during which the results of the feudal system made themselves felt. Wars between fiefs were henceforward impossible. But the bigger vassals were still powerful enough to hire troops and to support policies of their own. ⟨The Praguerie under Charles VI, the League of the Common Weal under Louis XI, and the "Crazy War" under Charles VIII all served to check the royal power.⟩ A century later France was to be so shaken by the Wars of Religion that influential men like Condé, Montmorency, Guise, the Princes of the Blood, Anjou, Alençon, Navarre, aided by the heat of passions, were able to recruit armies. ⟨Things came to such a pass during the minority of Louis XIII and, for the last time, during the Fronde, that the great nobles waged private wars at the head of their own troops.⟩ This, however, was nothing but the last writhings of a dying order. The fury of the Swiss mercenaries, followed by the death of Charles the Bold, marked the end of the Burgundian army. That of Brittany melted away at Saint-Aubin-du-Cormier. When Constable Bourbon took up arms against Francis I he was looked on as a traitor. ⟨Henry IV had only to hear mass and to sign the Edict of Nantes to bring about the end of the civil war between the League and the Protestants.⟩ A little later the heads which fell at Richelieu's behest afforded ample proof that no weapons could any longer avail against those of the king. As for the Fronde, its sole supporters were the *Parlement* of Paris, ten thousand nobles and a handful of prelates.

⟨As national unity became more and more a reality, the country's ambitions, which hitherto had been centred upon internal strife, were directed abroad.⟩ The wounds of the Hundred Years' War healed rapidly. France, prosperous and prolific, disputed the claims of Maximilian in Flanders, marched to the conquest of Italy, held the balance of power against Charles V, supported the Stuarts, and rounded off her frontiers. Despite grave disorders which emptied the treasury time and time again, the reforms enacted by Jacques Coeur and Louis XI provided public finance with a stability which allowed the country to support the costs of war. In principle military expenses were covered by the *taille* or poll-tax. There were, it is true, abuses enough, delays and waste. "No more money, no more Swiss", was often a literal description of the situation. Only too often the *lansquenets* (German *landsknechts*: soldiers of fortune) had to find their own pay. The Gascons regretted bitterly at times that they had accepted service in the king's army. All the same, Charles VII had forty thousand soldiers on his pay-roll, while Charles VIII and Louis XII both led sixty thousand men into Italy. Francis I had even more troops under his command when he undertook the conquest of Milan. When, in 1536, Charles V invaded Picardy, Provence, and Languedoc, he was opposed by over a hundred thousand soldiers. With an equal number Henry II was able to capture the three Bishoprics of Metz, Toul, and Verdun, and to wage campaigns in Lorraine, Piedmont, and the Pyrenees at the same time. Equal numbers were used by the various factions in the Wars of Religion; and although, in view of the country's exhaustion, Henry IV and Sully decided to disband part of the army, Richelieu found no difficulty in bringing it up to strength. ⟨It would be true to say that between the Hundred Years' and the Thirty Years' Wars, France was served by the finest army in the world.⟩

⟨Like technical development in general, the changes in armaments tended towards the creation of a regular professional army.⟩ Firearms were undergoing constant improvements. The iron bombards with their stone cannon-balls were soon displaced by bronze cannon hurling metal projectiles. From the end of the fifteenth century both light artillery, such as falcons and sakers, and heavier pieces such as culverins, possessed enough power and mobility to make them formidable weapons, provided they were capably handled. It soon became evident, too, that, with the help of gunpowder, a portable metal tube projecting bullets would be more effective than bows with arrows or bolts. The arquebus was the result. The priming was fired by a match grasped between the jaws of a nipping apparatus or *serpentin*, the weapon being supported by a fork stuck into the ground, and serving to absorb the recoil. The effect of fire in its turn brought about modifications in the division of the different arms, in the tactics governing their employment, either alone or in combination with other arms. Tavannes was able to say that in his own century "no art has suffered so many changes as the art of war; so much so that books and precepts are no longer useful after thirty years".

As befitted its prestige, the cavalry was the first arm to be reorganized as a striking force. From the time of Charles VII the cavalry unity, or "lance", consisted of one man-at-arms, three bowmen, a cutler, and a page, all mounted and armed. A hundred lances formed a company, whose commander was nominated by the king. Gradually the cavalry was divided up into three sections: the *gendarmerie*, clad in magnificent armour purchased at a high price in Milan, and wielding the twelve-foot lance and the two-edged sword; then the light cavalry—known as *reîtres* if they came from Germany—wearing the half-cuirass and armed with a shorter weapon than the lance—with the pistol from the reign of Francis I onwards; and companies of scouts and arquebusiers to reconnoitre and skirmish ahead of the main body.

Great as was the progress of the cavalry, the infantry became the masters of the battlefield. This was partly, no doubt, a result of the general improvement in social conditions. During the fifteenth and sixteenth centuries there was a notable decline in poverty, ignorance and servitude, and the enhanced conditions of the masses was reflected in their military achievements. But the foot-soldier owed his new power and dignity, unheard of in feudal times, to the fact that he was a professional soldier equipped with deadly weapons. The infantry had already shown during the Hundred Years' War that it could combine mobility with bowmanship to great effect. By crushing the Burgundians the cantonal detachments demonstrated the tremendous stability possessed by well-disposed and well-trained foot-soldiers. The Swiss mercenaries with their long pikes formed mobile "hedgehogs" able to withstand the fiercest charge and capable of piercing the enemy lines. During a period of a hundred and fifty years the tendency was to increase progressively the proportion of firearms among the infantry, to develop the cohesion of the pikemen and, above all, to co-ordinate even the smallest units of both arms. The natural consequence of these reforms was the creation of permanent tactical formations.

In point of fact the infantry did not come into its own without a struggle. At first governments were chary about committing themselves to such an expensive item as a permanent body of foot-soldiers. Would there not always be time, in an emergency, to hire those who were ready and waiting in foreign countries? There were the Swiss mercenaries, famous throughout the whole of Europe since Granson and Morat, ready to auction themselves to the Emperor, the King of France, Venice, the Pope or Piedmont; there were the *lansquenets* provided by the German princes who made a regular industry of training and hiring them out; there were Flemings and Brabants, once employed by the dukes of Burgundy, but now available to the highest bidder. Moreover, why give up the old militia which supplied foot-soldiers so cheaply? It was an easy matter to muster the "free archers" from every parish and, as Francis I was to do subsequently, to form seven provincial legions, each of six thousand men. But it gradually became evident that it is not possible to make a reliable body of infantry out of a thousand bits and pieces. The Swiss, it is true, brave, tough and battle-trained, rendered magnificent service. At Fornovo, Agnadello, and

Cérisoles they took a large share in the French success and losses. But at La Bicocca and on the Sesia they proved so unreasonable, sullen and touchy that they put their employers into dire straits. At Marignano they suffered a defeat at the hands of the king's troops which brought them to reason. But they took their revenge at Pavia. The *lansquenets*, on the other hand, fought willingly enough for the French. But these worthy sons of the Palatinate, Swabia, and Westphalia were for ever asking for increases in pay. What is more, they were past-masters in the art of plunder. So long as the fighting was done in Italy the king tolerated this behaviour, but when the campaign moved to Champagne or Picardy the case was altered. Moreover, Charles V was to expel Germans serving the enemy from the Empire. This raised difficulties in recruiting, soon to be further complicated by questions of religion. Meanwhile Spain, suzerain of the Low Countries since the death of Charles the Bold, was anxious to keep for herself the services of the Brabants and the Flemings. When it is added that after the Free Archers had been crushed by Maximilian at Guinegate owing to their lack of organization, the remnants had to be sent home, and that the Legionaries, apathetic and badly trained, fought badly and deserted *en masse*, it will be realized that force of circumstances gradually compelled France to constitute a national force of regular infantry.

The work was already begun by Louis XI. In 1481 at the camp of Pont de l'Arche he ordered d'Esquerdes and William Picquart to muster twenty thousand seasoned foot-soldiers of France to be formed into regular troops. These goodly companies subsequently garrisoned the towns on the Somme, this river then forming the French frontier, and later became the "Picardy Bands". Anne de Beaujeu made use of them during her regency to prevent Maximilian from invading French territory during Charles VIII's minority. Later, the attempts of Charles V against the eastern provinces led Francis I to complete the bands of Picardy by those of "Champagne". Meanwhile, Louis XII brought into existence the "Bands of Piedmont" to form the nucleus of the infantry to be used beyond the Alps. "Piedmont" recruited chiefly Gascons, Provençals, and Basques, as well as those Corsicans who were "law-abiding and conscious of their duties"; "Picardy" and "Champagne", on the other hand, drew their recruits chiefly from the northern provinces. In this way two bodies of infantry were formed in France, each with its own characteristics; the northerners heavier and tough, dependable and somewhat dour; the southerners quicker, more adaptable, mercurial and high-spirited. These distinctions were destined to remain; the armies of the Rhine have always been different in character from the armies of Italy.

For general purposes the company was the unit. When the troops went into action the army corps, known as "battles", were subdivided into "battalions". But it was not until much later that François de Guise formed "regiments", so great was the fear of putting an organically constituted military force into the hands of any individual. The first regiments were, naturally, "Picardy", "Piedmont" and "Champagne". They were followed by "Guyenne", "Navarre", and the "French Guards". Charles IX had three regiments, Henry IV eleven, Louis XIII thirty. For centuries operations and administration were to work together with the same unit, though without any excess of mutual esteem.

Whereas the infantry was to have such a chequered existence, the artillery found its organization from the outset. Depending as it does on its equipment, it is not a suitable medium for experiments. A corps of artillery was created forthwith. Its commanders, the brothers Bireau, the two Genouillacs, Langières, Cossé-Brissac, d'Estrées, Sully, enjoyed the constant support of the king. Although the French were slow to appreciate the importance of artillery, they showed great perseverance in developing it, once they were converted. For one thing, the Crown soon realized the power conferred on it by cannon, while, on the other hand, the element of mathematics involved appealed to the French mind. In fact, the artillery of Charles VII and of Louis XI had already played a leading part at Formigny, Castillon, Saint-Aubin, and Montlhéry. It was responsible, according to Mathieu de Cousay, for placing all the towns of Burgundy and Flanders in the king's hands. Charles VIII brought a hundred and forty heavy guns and over two thousand light pieces to Italy, "to the great amazement of the inhabitants". In later years there was no great increase in the numbers of cannon put into the line, but improvements in the founding, manufacture, and calibration of guns and projectiles, as well as in the manufacture of powder and in methods of laying and loading, rendered their fire increasingly powerful, accurate and rapid. After twenty shots at a range of six hundred paces the bombard of Crécy was out of action. A hundred years later, an average cannon could fire sixty cannon-balls an hour. Given a few shots, a good marksman could hit the target at two thousand feet. The mobility of artillery was increased by providing the cannon with limbers, by improving the wheels, gun-carriages, ammunition waggons and the system of haulage. In Henry II's reign the artillery was organized on a permanent basis by standardizing the "six royal calibres" of field artillery and by organizing the baggage "train".

But changes were to follow not only in the character of the troops but in that of the command. In former times a lord went into battle at the head of his own troops; now all troops without exception owed allegiance to the king. Ranks, therefore, became officers, and a corps of officers came into existence. The nobility, it is true, still provided the majority of officers, and a great name still counted, especially as the local influence of the aristocracy was found useful for recruiting purposes—a consideration which tended to make royal policy favour the great families. The royal princes remained, as before, generals by right of birth. Nevertheless, army rank gradually ceased to be a question of prerogative and became instead a career. The desire to excel was reinforced by a spirit of subordination: a leader was less anxious to appear as a "proud baron" than as a "loyal servant".

This union of the old knightly spirit with the new idea of discipline was to produce a brilliant galaxy of leaders. In like manner the finest crops spring from the best-ploughed land. A host of first-rate captains was to give the standing army its indispensable backbone. Men like Bayard, Louis d'Ars, La Cropte, Mollard, and, later, Montluc, Biron, La Noue and many others like them, or anxious to emulate them, were loyal and honourable men whose ideal still remained the individual escapade, but who made it a point of honour to carry out their orders. Soldiers such as these, children of a hot-blooded century, nurtured by a prodigal motherland, displayed miracles of valour and ingenuity, at Naples, on the Ebro or the Rhine, without counting the cost. Bayard died on the battlefield in his thirty-seventh year, having fought in nineteen campaigns and eighty battles.

As for leaders like d'Esquerdes, La Trémoille, Bonnivet, La Palice, Lautrec, Brissac, Montmorency, Termes, Strozzi, Coligny, Saint-André, Tavannes, whether their high office was the result of birth or service or the turn of events, they showed themselves brave and inured to battle, good judges of the enemy and of their own troops. The princes, Gaston de Foix, Enghien, the Guises and Condés, presuming upon their youth, their birth and their reputation, snapped their fingers in the face of fate. As for the kings, they took command in all the principal theatres of war, and gave proof of brilliant military qualities. The Valois took readily to warfare and were quick to realize how much their presence could do to stiffen wavering loyalties. Despite his infirmities, Louis XI was present at more than one engagement. Throughout the Italian campaigns Charles VIII, Louis XII, and Francis I took charge of operations. In the struggle against Charles V, Henry II put himself at the head of his troops in Lorraine and Champagne. The Princes of the Blood, constables and marshals of France, followed their king's example and did not hesitate to risk their own skins. La Trémoille and La Palice were killed at Pavia, Gaston de Foix at Ravenna, Termes at Gravelines, Strozzi at the siege of Thionville, François de Guise near Orleans, Saint-André at Dreux, Joyeuse at Coutras and Condé at Boussac. The wound of which Montmorency, Constable of France, died at Saint-Denis was the eighth he had received during sixty years of active service. Their opponents, men like the Duke of Alba, the Duke of Savoy, Count Egmont, Ferdinand of Gonzago, William and, later, Maurice of Nassau, all showed the same distinction. And yet on neither side did leaders emerge who, by bending war to their own wills, were able to exploit its manifold combinations to obtain results of the first magnitude.

It must be realized that armies of those days were crippled by sheer weight. The arquebus weighed fifty pounds, exclusive of powder and shot. The ten-foot pike was no lighter. In addition, the foot-soldier carried a sword or dagger at his side, often a helmet on his head, while his body was weighed down by layer upon layer of leather and steel. When one takes into account the weight of provisions, cloak, shield and, in many cases, the trenching tool, one realizes what the unfortunate infantry had to carry with them on the march. The mounted gendarmerie were scarcely mobile beneath their coat of armour. Their horses were so heavily loaded that they could jump a fence only with the greatest difficulty. The artillery was able to get along at a jog-trot on roads fit for wheeled traffic, but once off the roads the cannons and limbers soon became bogged. Moreover, neither men-at-arms nor mercenaries would consent to do without a thousand-and-one comforts, with the result that the troops were followed by a mass of transport carrying food as well as military supplies. The fact that armies rarely left the roads, which, in any case, were few and in bad repair, endowed the places commanding the roads with a rôle of capital importance. Hence the long and costly sieges. A constant struggle was waged between artillery and fortifications, which, under the influence of Italian engineers, were given rounded lines offering little hold to artillery bombardment. In its turn, the artillery increased in power and precision until it was able to breach the stoutest walls.

If straightforward marches presented such difficulties, it is easy to imagine the slowness of manœuvres. Scouts, whether mounted or on foot, could scour the country easily enough; but whole infantry battalions, companies of men-at-arms, batteries and convoys were hard put to it to make any headway over hills and dales, across meadow and ploughland, through woods and vineyards. The greatest care was needed in choosing suitable terrain for deploying troops or giving battle. The commander-in-chief and the camp marshals were faced with the extraordinarily difficult task of marshalling the troops, for the value of the infantry depended on its battle-array; the cavalry was helpless on ground unsuitable for the charge; the artillery had to be placed and protected by earthworks once and for all; while the extremely vulnerable convoys were not only a tempting target for the enemy, but a cause of anxiety for their various owners.

As the two opposing sides approached each other there were skirmishes between the foremost elements on the flanks. The first care of the attackers was to mop up the host of stragglers, a task usually left to the cavalry. The operation was fraught with perils: an excess of enthusiasm or, more simply, booby-traps might easily lead the horsemen into an ambush. But in any case, once the main body of the enemy troops was located, the moving shield of horsemen divided, uncovering the infantry behind.

Cautiously, with their pikes held high, protected by swarms of crossbowmen, the leading battalions advanced, dragging along with them a few light cannon. The crisis was reached when the first shots were fired. Bullets and cannon-balls cut deep lanes through the opposing ranks of footmen, who could neither scatter nor lie down, for fear of the cavalry. Captains in front, lieutenants on the flanks and the *serre-files* who brought up the rear, endeavoured by every available means to keep each man in his place. Every now and then a halt was called to re-form ranks, to gather in the rovers and allow the artillery to make itself heard in its turn. But if, despite every care, it should happen that the enemy cavalry came on, with lances lowered, at the gallop, then, quickly, the square had to be formed, or all was lost. Then, packed tight behind the bristling forest of their lances, the infantry waited for the storm to pass.

At last comes the moment for the death-grapple. The crossbowmen make way. At the word of command, the pikemen, gripping their pikes with both hands, bend their heads and bodies forward to support their weapons. Then with a mighty growl and shouts of "Forward! Thrust! Follow up!" the infantry dashes with a tremendous roar into the enemy line.

The assault may force the enemy to abandon his defensive positions. At Granson, the Burgundian infantry, attacked by the Swiss mercenaries on the outskirts of its encampment, fled at the first shock of arms. At Guinegate, when Maximilian went over to the offensive, his Flemish troops dispersed the French militia with their first charge. Sometimes, however, the defenders would recoil only to unmask their hidden batteries and to make a surprise counter-attack. The Genoese of the "Promontory", who attacked the French lines as they thought victoriously, were routed in this manner. There were other instances where the two opposing forces of infantry became locked in a death-struggle: at Novaro, for example, where the Swiss mercenaries of Milan met the *lansquenets* of Louis XII. In any case, once the enemy's formation has been broken up by fire, or by the charge or by obstacles, the attacking cavalry is quickly on the scene driving in the flanks with lance and sword, or harassing the front with arquebus and pistol, endeavouring by every means to produce among the infantry a state of panic which will make it an easy prey for the horsemen.

So the battle develops, in many cases split up into isolated struggles in which the decisive factor is the enterprise and energy of individual leaders. An advance here, a withdrawal there, casualties, fatigue, mistakes, combine to dislocate an army's dispositions. There are so many breaches and scrimmages that any sudden event may upset the whole equilibrium. The moment has come for the general with reserves to throw them into the battle. This is, in fact, what happened at Morat when, towards the end of the day, Hans de Hallwyl's Swiss Corps overwhelmed the right wing of the Burgundians, broke through into their camp and captured their artillery. At Cérisoles, the Count of Enghien, exploiting a false move on the part of the Neapolitan light horse, rallied his cavalry and broke through the line of Spanish infantry. At Fauquembergues the victory was decided by the unexpected charge of the French gendarmerie against the exhausted army of the Duke of Savoy. When this happened, the vanquished had little hope of recovery; to flee was to court disaster. The knights, it is true, were able to dig in their spurs and save their skins. But the foot-soldiers, throwing down their arms in order to run faster, offered an easy prey to the victorious cavalry. Occasionally, whole battalions which, despite everything, had managed to keep their formation, did succeed in retreating either under cover of darkness or thanks to a momentary respite during which the enemy gave up the pursuit in order to plunder the baggage train. But sometimes, isolated and surrounded by enemies, maddened by suffering, like Romagnes' infantry at Agnadel, the Spanish "tercios" at Ravenna, or the old French trainbands on the evening of Saint Lawrence's day, they put up a last fight. Then, pounded by the artillery, exposed to musket-fire from every side, charged without mercy or quarter, they died on the "bed of honour".

In the military sphere, as in all others, the Renaissance paved the way for the classical period. Though war may not yet have become the perfect instrument which, later, was to serve the genius of Gustavus Adolphus, the talent of Turenne, or, finally, the art of Frederick, yet it contained at least the germs of the future masterpiece. In any case, from its very beginnings, the standing army succeeded in protecting and strengthening France. It is true that, to build the edifice, a certain amount of inferior matter, or even rubbish, had to be mixed with the finest material in the country. But war has the virtue of ennobling even the vilest.

ANCIEN RÉGIME

I

THE POLICY OF SEVENTEENTH-CENTURY FRANCE WAS FORMED BY CIRCUMSTANCES. It fought shy of abstractions, preferring facts to fancies, usefulness to sublimity, and opportunism to glory. For each particular problem it sought the practical rather than the ideal solution. Though unscrupulous as to the means employed, it showed its greatness by keeping a nice proportion between the end in view and the resources of the state.

What was true of policy was true of its instrument, the army. Its recruitment and its organization were based not on law but on experiment. Its discipline and its code of honour were based on fact rather than theory. Strategy and tactics took as their guide common sense, experience and a wise opportunism, unhampered by formulae.

The wars of the period rarely aroused great national enthusiasm. Revolution in the Low Countries, the hostility of the Dutch, the union of the Rhineland towns, the English Revolution, the succession to the Spanish and Polish thrones, the strength of Prussia, the extent of France's colonial empire—all these things exercised the minds of Frenchmen. But none of the resulting struggles seemed to provide justification for tearing peasants away from their fields, craftsmen from their benches, or citizens from their businesses or public offices. Saint-Germain was accurately expressing the general opinion when he said: "It is not seemly to destroy the nation in order to form armies." The majority of Frenchmen, therefore, were to be allowed to live their lives peacefully. Only a few of them would be required to fight.

But which were they to be? In this seventeenth-century society a host of privileges, contracts and traditions limited, complicated, and modified the rights of each social group: class, province, township, statutory body or corporation. On whatever category of citizens compulsory military service had been imposed, the whole fabric of society would have been rent from top to bottom. Recruits were provided, therefore, by those isolated individuals whose absence would inconvenience nobody: young men with a distaste for a humdrum existence on the farm, in the shop or counting-house, and a taste for adventure and uniform; down-and-outs, ready to exchange their liberty for food and clothing; bad characters with little choice in life except that between military service or the gallows. Each colonel was responsible for finding recruits for his own regiment. Recruiting was a specialized profession, using methods varying from persuasion, with or without intoxication, to intimidation. Nevertheless, the abuses must not be too patent: "His Majesty," runs an order of Louvois, "finds it good that small irregularities be concealed. Only violence and kidnapping from fairgrounds and markets are forbidden."

On the same principle, the maximum possible number of foreigners was pressed into service. Some joined up of their own accord, having been driven from their homes by the harshness of economic conditions. Among such were many Germans, Belgians, Swedes, Poles, Danes, and Hungarians. Others were lent under contract by their governments. Such were the Swiss, provided for the king of France by virtue of the "Capitulations" of Francis I with the Cantons; the Piedmontese, presented by Savoy; the Rhinelanders, Bavarians, and

Swabians dispatched by their respective princes. Others, like the English regiments which had come over with the Stuarts or the Irish Brigade of James II, fought as auxiliaries. When Louis XIV gave orders for the invasion of Holland, he had 45,000 foreign to 80,000 French foot-soldiers, whilst half his horsemen, that is 20,000 men, had been recruited from outside the national frontiers. This explains why Louis never allowed the term "the French army", but only "the army of France". According to a contemporary witness: "In the king's eyes a foreign soldier is worth three men. He's one man less for the enemy and one more in our ranks. Moreover, he's one more Frenchman that can be left on the land or in the workshop."

The army in the field, therefore, consisted of pressed men from inside the country and foreign mercenaries. And pre-Revolution France was quite content with this type of recruiting. Its irregularity and poor quality were admitted, and, on occasions, corrected. But the method was retained as weighing less heavily on the nation than any other. It was considered good in so far as it was adequate for its purpose.

But the country had to be prepared for any eventuality. If the existence of France were imperilled by a foreign enemy, she could count upon a national armed rising. The Monarchy was fully conscious that the country was saved in this way at Bouvines and at Mons-la-Puelle. So it carefully preserved the ancient institution of the regional militias, in which the soldiers, recruited by parishes, were formed into companies and regiments under the command of retired officers or of officers on furlough. This militia provided garrisons for towns, kept watch on the frontiers between the bodies of regular troops, helped to maintain order, tracked down deserters, escorted convoys and guarded prisoners. Their duties, which were usually inglorious, roused little enthusiasm among the militiamen, and the organization remained unpopular so long as its usefulness was not apparent as a matter of urgency. But when, in 1709, the Allies had advanced into Hainault and Flanders, and, after capturing Lille, were preparing to march on Paris, the militia, which went into action at Malplaquet, acquitted themselves valiantly.

The king employed the same empirical methods in his choice of officers. The nobility had a taste for and the tradition of war. Its members were accustomed by social circumstances to command. The custom whereby the family property and responsibilities passed to the eldest son tended to drive the younger sons into the army. Moreover, the France of Louis XIV had just emerged from a succession of crises in which both the royal authority and national unity had been imperilled by the turbulence and the ambition of the nobility. The government had every reason, therefore, to urge this class to fight the enemies of France. And finally, the nobles were in possession of wealth which, by skilful management, might be made to benefit the whole army. The nobles provided, in fact, the majority of the officers.

To foster the loyalty of the greatest among them, and to turn to advantage their prestige, and even their wealth, the king began by selling them the right to form regiments and companies of their own and to dress, equip and feed them. In this way a youth of noble birth found himself captain or colonel as soon as he reached man's estate. If, in action, he gave proof of military aptitude, he might later become one of the great leaders.

Those, whether noble or bourgeois, of more modest birth served as young men with the musketeers of the King's Household, or else in the cadets or Military School. They left with an officer's commission and, having gained a little experience, they purchased a company. From that moment onwards their future depended entirely on themselves and their stars. In many cases they were killed or maimed in action. Others, after twenty or thirty years' service, retired as captains, majors or lieutenant-colonels into their native province, more or less crippled with wounds, but rich in heroic and picturesque memories which they were fond of telling to their nephews, or even of committing to paper. Some became brigadiers, camp marshals, lieutenants-general or marshals of France. In such cases, loaded with glory, titles and pensions, they looked back wistfully upon their youth with its fruitful illusions.

The difficulty of disciplining an army of this kind may readily be imagined. These hotheads, ne'er-do-wells and vagabonds turned soldiers were not docile by nature. Some of them had no scruples about deserting, thereby breaking a contract into which they had been hoodwinked by fear or ignorance. Unless drastic measures had been taken, the troops would soon have been ruined by the chances of pillage and plunder and other misdemeanours afforded by a campaign. The pains and penalties with which they were threatened were terrible indeed. Yet, despite everything, as soon as the opportunity presented itself, the troops melted into thin air. In the expedition to Sicily in 1677 Marshal de Vivonne discovered in the course of an inspection of the infantry that four thousand out of seven thousand men had deserted. At the time of the war with Holland, Louvois, writing to Luxemburg, stated: "Letters from Nijmegen apprise me that over two thousand French deserters have passed through the place." The fearful punishments incurred by the bad soldiers were, in fact, rarely enforced. As a rule, when, willingly or not, the deserters had rejoined their unit, they were pardoned in the hope of making good soldiers of them. "Desertion," we read in an order of the day of 1666, "has become so habitual among the troops that there are few soldiers who have not fallen into this criminal practice."

Nor was it easy to obtain regular service and obedience from the officers. Richelieu and Mazarin had lopped off the last branches from the tree of feudal independence, but the roots remained deeply embedded in the soil. The nobles, who were exemplary in their courage on the battlefield or in the trenches, found their other military obligations irksome. No sooner had the army taken up its quarters than many of the leaders went home or to court, leaving the troops in the charge of a few so-called "officers of fortune"—though they were possessed of none. Moreover, the rank bestowed by virtue of birth and fortune conferred but little authority on men of real worth, while, conversely, the latter, placed in positions of authority, found it difficult to exact obedience from men of higher nobility or from those more favoured than themselves at court. The great leaders themselves failed to give an example of subordination. Several of them, notably Condé and Turenne, had previously taken up arms against the royal authority. Each of them, jealous of the others, claimed the privilege of independence for himself.

This lack of discipline among soldiers and officers would have ruined the French army of the *ancien régime* if there had not been a Minister who, while making allowances for what was inevitable, did everything in his power to check it. Brought up by his father, Le Tellier, in the tradition of those great servants of the state who owed their advancement to merit and held their positions as a reward for services rendered, Louvois, during thirty years of office, worked hard and tirelessly, showing at the same time his strong will and his discrimination. Disdainful of theories, he was careful not to disrupt and destroy; as a realist he was persistent in his efforts to reform and improve. Though obstinate in pursuing his ends, he was nevertheless capable of flexibility. An enthusiastic planner, he knew how to bide his time. Unfettered by scruples, he used whatever means appeared simplest and most expedient. Though severe in his judgments of men, he did not despise them. He was clear-sighted without scepticism, devoid of illusions but not of faith; and although hard on inefficiency and pitiless towards pretentiousness, he was ungrudging in his recognition and encouragement of talent. He was reserved without being unapproachable, prepared to read reports but firm in forming his own judgment, welcoming advice but reserving the final decision for himself. He had enemies and allies, but no friends. Living only for his work, revelling in power, prodigal with time—the stuff of great endeavour—patient and daring, active and cautious, thorough and practical at the same time, Louvois was the ideal Minister of War for the *ancien régime*.

In order to discipline his troops Louvois set out to provide them with the kind of life which induced discipline. Every corps, clothed hitherto according to the personal ideas of the colonel, was required to don the king's uniform. Weapons must conform to regulations. To remedy the notoriously inconvenient system of billeting soldiers on private individuals, Louvois brought into being the first barracks, which he was careful to place on the outskirts of the towns. The barracks in Paris bearing the names of Lourcine, Pépinière, Courtille, Babylone, Roule, and Courbevoie all date from this period. Louvois ordered frequent changes of garrisons and, to ensure that the moves were carried out smoothly, mapped out the routes and stages in advance. He introduced into the army a system of compulsory instruction, creating for the infantry, cavalry, and artillery a body of inspectors who reviewed the troops and were present on exercises and manœuvres. To Louvois the army owes the practice of marching in step and of arms drill. Pay, which hitherto had been fixed by a so-called agreement between the captain and the recruit, was made uniform, while war commissioners were appointed to see that it reached the men. Louvois transformed the conditions under which the soldiers lived while on active service by organizing stores and quarters before operations were undertaken. As soon as the common soldier realized that he would draw his pay regularly and find billets prepared for him, he was much less inclined to desert or plunder.

It would have been futile to expect discipline from the soldiers if the officers did not set the example: Louvois, therefore, undertook to compel them to do so. In time of war they were to be with their units from one end of the campaign to the other. There were to be no more of those casual commanders who turned up on the eve of the battle and departed the day after. Once the king had announced the opening of the campaign, every officer was obliged to remain at his post with the army until it went into winter quarters. Then, and only then, could he return home, visit his property, hunt, settle his accounts with the farmers, or run off to Versailles to catch the eye of the king and of the "best people", show himself during the winter season, and acquire from the smiles of the ladies, the compliments of friends or the discomfiture of jealous rivals the requisite amount of *amour-propre* to carry him through the following year's campaign. Henceforward an officer could leave the service only if his resignation had been regularly tendered and accepted. In peacetime he was required to put in a minimum number of appearances and was held responsible for his troops during his time of absence. Any dereliction of duty on his part was liable to be sharply pointed out by the inspectors or by the Minister himself, who reprimanded or punished the guilty with no light hand. Whatever an officer's rank or birth or protection, he was required to obey. When Martinet, the Inspector-General of Infantry, showed signs of reluctance in rebuking certain high-born officers, Louvois wrote in these terms: "Tell them that the first man of them to disobey orders will be cashiered." On another occasion he wrote: "The King desires you to imprison the first officer who makes difficulties." When a certain General Montil raised objections and spoke of resigning in the middle of the campaign, Louvois wrote to his Commander-in-Chief as follows: "I believe Montil to be too intelligent to ask me for permission to resign, because it is the direct path to the Bastille, where the King habitually consigns those who make such requests to him."

But Louvois did more than demand obedience; he took steps to make obedience easier to give. In order to increase the part played in promotion by merit, he created the ranks of major and lieutenant-colonel which might be bestowed on officers who were too poor to purchase a regiment, and which led directly to the rank of general. He inaugurated "promotion lists", and saw to it that promotions were decided accordingly. To make it possible for the less wealthy nobles to enter the exclusive corps of Musketeers or of the King's Household, Louvois founded schools in which cadets could qualify as cornets, ensigns or lieutenants.

However dictatorial he might be by nature, Louvois showed considerable skill and flexibility in his dealings with the great captains of his day. His procedure varied according to the personality of his man. The great Condé, a Prince of the Blood, covered with glory and ripe in experience, would never have taken advice from the young Secretary of State. Louvois was clever enough to make it appear that any suggestion he had to make came in fact from Condé himself. With the cold and haughty Turenne, who in his dealings with the Minister showed the very natural impatience of overbearing characters when faced with men of their own stamp, Louvois adopted the method of going straight to the point. But with Vauban he could reason. He knew that this great soldier was disinterested, resourceful and endowed with common sense, and more likely than anyone else to throw light upon a problem. His bluntest speech was reserved for Luxemburg, the great lord consumed by ambition and vice, but exceptionally gifted; the Minister was treated in turn to extremes of flattery or insolence. The steady, thoughtful Catinat, on the other hand, had to be prodded, for, though methodical in preparing and determined in executing a plan, he was apt to be moody and vacillating and unwilling to undertake bold and vigorous actions. A factor which did much to inspire the loyalty of the marshals and to help to solve some of the thorny questions of precedence in the organization of the command was the frequent appearance of the King among his armies. Louvois, then, was able to impose his will, either by authority or diplomacy, by rough methods or gentle. But he put up with a certain amount of resistance and rebelliousness from the great leaders, realizing that this is but the usual accompaniment of strong personalities. As leaders of his armies he preferred strong if awkward characters to more manageable but less vigorous natures.

Despite the improvements introduced by Louvois, discipline remained imperfect. The great unifying bond of the army was military honour, in which self-respect and comradeship joined with devotion to the king, who was the embodiment of patriotism and chivalry. Every means was employed to evoke and foster the corporate spirit: illustrious names for regiments, brilliant uniforms—every corps had its own particular details, badges, and so on, of which it was jealously proud—carefully-preserved traditions and customs. In addition, many units possessed certain traditional privileges: the twelve oldest regiments, for example, enjoyed the privilege of fighting on the right wing of the infantry, while the Picardy regiments had the right of leading the attack. Several corps displayed the white standard at the head of their first company—the "colonel's company"; others had received their equipment from the king; others again had the "right of provost", that is to say, their men could be tried only by the provost of their own regiment. This team spirit, when exaggerated, became fanatical and intolerant. In 1644, at the siege of Gravelines, the regiments of the Guards and of Navarre quarrelled as to which one should be the first to enter the town. In the presence of their excited troops, the colonels drew their swords and fighting broke out between the soldiers, who were separated only with the greatest difficulty.

Picked units not only kept alive a spirit of emulation in the army, but often carried out special tactical tasks. The general reserve for battle consisted of troops of the King's Household, the Gendarmes of the Guard, the Light Horse, French Guards, Swiss Guards and Musketeers. In each infantry regiment the assault columns were led by companies of grenadiers. With the cavalry it was the duty of the carabiniers to cover the flanks during the charge. In order to combat staleness among the troops the *ancien régime* gave certain soldiers or certain picked units new weapons, with higher pay for those using them. It was in this way that it created musketeers when the musket replaced the arquebus, grenadiers when grenades came into use, carabiniers when the cavalry had to be reconciled to the use of firearms, fusiliers when the decision was made to replace the musket by the rifle, and bombardiers when artillery began to be organized on a regular footing. There was great competition to get into one of these privileged units. At the siege of Monthéliard in 1694 General Catinat had a young soldier brought before him who had just performed an act of gallantry, and asked him what reward he would like. "Let me join a grenadier company, sir," replied the soldier.

Nor was the soldier's individual pride forgotten. Ceremonial parades with flourish of trumpets, public commendation, stripes, long-service medals gratified the valiant soldier and the veteran. Officers received the Order of St. Louis, or, if they were Protestants, the Order of Military Merit. In addition, every soldier might have his name entered on the pensions list.

So long as he lived and fought in the ranks, the soldier of the *ancien régime* was supported by a soldier's honour. But at last wounds and age, or else the demobilization which follows every war, obliges him to leave the service. What is to become of him in that civilian life with which he has no links? The king will grant him a small pension, it is true. No doubt, too, his adventurous life has taught him how to make the best of circumstances; he will have brought home from the Low Countries, Germany, Italy, America or India a host of soldiers' tales which will not fail to find a willing—and sometimes a generous—audience in the parks and taverns of the town. Then many a great lord or wealthy merchant will be glad to engage this respectable old soldier as a house-porter, many a convent will take him to look after the garden and serve mass, and will endeavour to cure him of his bad language by the ministrations of tobacco. But in many cases he cannot adapt himself to this kind of life. He needs the atmosphere of the army with its comradeship and its regulations. In this case he goes to the Invalides, where he puts on uniform again, becomes part of a company, salutes his officers, obeys rules, lives among other soldiers and continues to enjoy the glamour of arms. It was Louvois, that stern War Minister, who, by founding the Invalides, made it possible for the soldier to end a life of hardship with honour.

The state certainly owed this care to the veterans from whom it demanded such great sacrifices. Not content with building its greatness upon their labours, it imbued both strategy and tactics with the spirit with which it was itself animated. It is true to say that at no other period of history was war more strictly subordinated to policy. Policy did not hesitate to unleash war, yet it never lost its grip on the reins, taking care to define its objective and to limit its scope. Warfare was never allowed to outstrip the exigencies of policy.

Governments were careful to limit the objectives at which they aimed. It is true that they strove incessantly to increase their territory, to support their allies and weaken their rivals, but they avoided great cataclysms and uncontrollable upheavals. Conscious of the nation's limited resources, they sought no hegemony. Since the enemy of today might be the friend of tomorrow, no adversary was to be crushed completely. But, on the other hand, no state must be allowed to grow too powerful. Above all, life must go on, and no useful purpose was served by unleashing between nations those wild ambitions, those unquenchable hatreds, which poison international relations and threaten world order.

In any case, the means at the government's disposal precluded grandiose enterprises. Soldiers were scarce and costly. They represented assets which must not be squandered. So long as it was possible to guarantee regular pay and properly organized lodging, so long as the troops could be moved by easy stages, it was possible to maintain discipline. But as soon as the army was far from its supplies, billeted at random and travelling through unknown country, the conscripts began to desert and plunder, whilst the mercenaries mutinied.

Strategy, too, was determined by the political end in view and by the means at the government's disposal. The *ancien régime* was not concerned with gigantic onslaughts aiming at the total destruction of the enemy, with grandiose schemes of invasion or with the desperate resistance of the whole nation. The war effort consisted in capturing or defending key towns, in brushing aside the enemy's forces at the smallest possible cost, in penetrating far enough into his territory to bring him to terms, in preventing opposing coalitions from joining forces, in reinforcing an ally, in bringing pressure to bear upon a neutral, or in laying waste the territory of an ill-disposed state. Battles were still fought in close formation; movement was slow and formal. For although cannon in the fifteenth century and muskets in the sixteenth had become effective weapons, the rate of fire was still slow and the range short. A cannon could fire one shot per minute at twelve hundred yards. A musket had a range of a hundred yards, and a skilful marksman could fire one shot in forty seconds, provided, that is, that neither the powder nor the flint was damped by rain and that the wind did not blow out the match. If the enemy against whom the army was advancing held his ground, the musketeers were obliged to withdraw in order to prepare their next volley. If the pikemen, with their formidable eighteen-foot weapon, had kept formation, the musketeers would shelter behind them. The battalion had, therefore, to be in close formation, with the pikemen in the centre and with a wing of musketeers on either side. In any case, these professional soldiers, grouped in units with jealously preserved traditions, could not have been drawn up in any other way. Battle array was prescribed to the last detail with a scrupulous respect for the "normal order" and the prerogatives of the various units.

If formation was broken during the battle, the enemy cavalry, hovering on the flanks, would go over to the attack. Infiltrating through the gaps torn in the line of infantry, harassing it from the sides and in the rear, it quickly transformed confusion into a rout. It was therefore of the utmost importance to keep cohesion during the advance. At the Battle of the Dunes the French army formed up in its battle positions within a thousand yards of the Spanish army, and then took three hours to reach the enemy, because the dunes made it necessary to re-form constantly.

Not that bold strokes were ruled out. Condé affords a striking proof to the contrary. How could the example of such a royal prince fail to inspire an army in which so many officers came from a high-spirited aristocracy and soldiers held their lives cheap, having nothing else to lose? Condé, who may at times have thrown prudence to the winds, always took his full share of danger. At Freiburg and at Nordlingen, smiling amidst the smoke, he led the infantry to the attack. After the battle of Bléneau, Turenne had only to see the headlong flight of the Royalist army to exclaim: "The Prince has arrived and is in command of the pursuit!" At the battle of Senef, as soon as he learned that the Prince of Orange was present, Condé placed himself at the head of his vanguard and led a frontal attack against his rival. In such situations, the infantry bore him no grudge, though aware of what his conduct would cost them. A legend grew up round his person. The soldiers told how the Prince threw his stick into the enemy ranks and went to retrieve it with his own hands. But it was the cavalry more especially, which, led by Condé, passing through the zone of fire of a battalion in five seconds, developed a tremendously powerful punch. At Rocroi, for example, the Prince, at the head of some cavalry squadrons, began by crushing the enemy's left, and then, making a turning movement round the Spanish army, attacked the right wing from the rear, turned against the infantry in the centre and charged it three times before breaking it, after his weapons had been thrice hit by musket-fire.

Condé's daring was not mere recklessness. His dislike of minutely detailed plans and protracted preparations sometimes put him in a difficult situation—at Lens, Freiburg and Senef, for example. But his faculties were sharpened by action and danger. [He had the gift which, according to the degree in which it is possessed, is variously termed knack or genius, of deciding quickly when and where to strike with the maximum effect. In war and peace he played for high stakes and won or lost in the grand manner.]

Nevertheless, Turenne's methods were better suited to a period which aimed at using restricted means to attain limited objectives. At Freiburg, Nordlingen, Arras, Sintzheim, and Turckheim, Turenne, sparing in his use of inadequate effectives and careful to maintain order among troops whose whole value lay therein, acted only after full and due reflection. Before deciding on the direction and scope of his operations he devoted an extraordinary amount of energy to gathering information. He insisted on complete reconnaissance (which he carried out in person and which, on the last occasion, at Salzbach, cost him his life), and on outposts placed so as to give him complete liberty of action. But once the position was clear, once he was armed with all the available knowledge of all the variable factors—enemy, ground, morale—he made up his mind quickly and acted.

Such was Turenne's method of making war, seeking only the results required by policy and calculating the outlay accordingly, without expecting more than could be gained by the means available. Though complex, his tactics were always opportune. If, in many instances, he preferred minor actions to full-scale battles, provided he could get the same advantages from them, he did not hesitate to give battle whenever this course would give him the results he wanted. In such cases he made the most meticulous preparations for the battle, which he fought with the utmost vigour. His exploitation of success was usually limited by the consideration that all that was asked of the enemy was his withdrawal, and that a relentless pursuit might produce a dangerous state of disorder among the pursuing troops. The importance the Marshal gave to fortified positions was based on the conviction that nothing was gained so long as they remained in the enemy's hands, protecting his supplies, controlling roads and harbouring garrisons ready to make sorties. By his nice adjustment of ends to means, his love of facts and his contempt for theories, Turenne gave to military art the stamp of the *Grand Siècle*. Other victories were more brilliant and more resounding than his, though few were more durable. His triumphs have lasted, as those seventeenth-century masterpieces of literature and architecture have lasted, thanks to the nobility of their conception and the regularity of their proportions.

II

The prevailing seventeenth-century philosophy was calculated to strengthen the military power of France. After the Wars of Religion and the Fronde the nation felt the need of law and order. The following century, however, saw the birth and development of ideas and emotions which were to sweep away the *ancien régime*, after undermining its foundations. As the logical consequence of this lack of stability, scepticism and corruption disintegrated loyalty and crippled authority.

The crisis did not leave the army unaffected. Signs of trouble had been evident during the War of the Austrian Succession. After Dettingen, Marshal de Noailles wrote to the King: "Our enemies (English and Hanoverians) owe the success of their tactics entirely to their discipline, a thing which is not to be seen among our troops." Maurice of Saxony, in a report made to d'Argenson before the battle of Fontenoy, says: "There is so much disorder and insubordination, that I have been obliged to take drastic action." "Our troops," wrote an officer, "entered Bohemia, Westphalia and Bavaria with good and complete equipment. They have returned exhausted by the prodigiously large numbers of losses among officers and men. Yet we have been in no regular engagement. The soldiers spend their time in pillage and take the first opportunity of getting out of their leader's sight in order to decamp."

The Seven Years' War revealed the full extent of the evil. A weak and negligent administration handed over the organization of supply to dishonest contractors, with the result that the ill-fed and ill-equipped soldiers deserted to live on plunder. The officers did likewise. On the day of Rosbach, the army of 18,000 men under Soubise lost 6,000 men who deserted and gave themselves up to the enemy. From India, Dupleix begged the home government to stop sending him "the lowest ruffians by way of soldiers". When Lally was about to take Madras, his soldiers refused to march. Saint-Germain, lieutenant-general in the army of Hanover, wrote in a fit of uncontrollable rage: "I command a band of thieves and ruffians who run away at the first shot and are always on the verge of mutiny." There is a case on record of eight officers being cashiered in one day. The aged Marshal de Belle-Isle, who witnessed the operations, was horrified by what he saw: "Disorder, insubordination and brigandage," he writes, "have reached alarming proportions. In all my fifty years of soldiering I have never seen anything like it!"

What is more, the commander-in-chief himself, Marshal Richelieu, the victor of Port Mahon and Kloster-Seven, cheerfully bore the name given to him by his men of *Père la Maraude* ("Old Plunderer"). Saint-Germain, too, who judged his soldiers with such severity, simply abandoned them in the middle of a retreat, when Richelieu was replaced by Clermont, on the grounds that, in his opinion, he was a better general than Clermont. His departure was termed "resignation" and that was the end of it. The King was surrounded by intrigues of which the military leaders were both the instigators and the victims.

Patronage and intrigue, undermining authority, forced the government to multiply the number of officers. Towards the end of the Seven Years' War, there were 650 generals and 16,000 officers on the active list for an army of 200,000 men. Every regiment had anything up to ten colonels who took command in turn for a day at a time. In such conditions discipline and the commander's responsibility became meaningless terms. The supply lines behind the army were cluttered with a mass of personal baggage. At Rosbach, for example, the Prussians captured 1,200 wagon-loads of officers' baggage. Officers left their troops on every possible occasion, and in any case as soon as the campaign was over. As one minister put it: "The main cause of the country's reverses is the disastrous habit which deprives the troops in peacetime of the officers who are to lead them in time of war."

It would have been surprising if French strategy and tactics had remained sound and realistic in such conditions. Formerly they had been based on well-defined objectives, dependable resources and, above all, experience. The gap was filled by theory. And while in the French army common sense gave way to dogma, discipline became a formality and personality was swamped by convention, in Prussia a great king was perfecting the art of war of the *ancien régime* by which Turenne and his peers had won such fame and France such benefits.

The policy of that uncompromising realist, the King of Prussia, was directed towards the attainment of limited objectives which were clearly defined and steadily pursued. Frederick's object in entering the war of the Austrian Succession was to take Silesia and make of Prussia a great state, while the stubborn struggle in which he then engaged for seven years had as its aim to preserve what he had already acquired. He did not for one moment dream of destroying his neighbours, any more than they wished to annihilate Prussia. Louis XV, Maria Theresa, Maximilian and Catherine were just as anxious as Frederick to keep the balance of power in Europe.

Frederick's strategy was classical in its opportunism and its limited resources. In the War of the Austrian Succession he threw his troops into Silesia, and, having conquered it, was glad to accept the armistice. Then, disturbed by the successes of Maria Theresa, he went to war again to defend his conquest. At Millwitz and Friedberg he struck hard blows, but without going beyond his objective. At the beginning of the Seven Years' War Frederick attempted to seize Bohemia because it would serve a useful purpose in keeping the Austrians at arm's length. The attack on Prague had no other end in view. When the army of the German Circles and the forces of Soubise invaded Saxony and Richelieu was victorious against the English in Hanover, Prussia was in danger of invasion. At Rosbach Frederick defeated the Circles and Soubise, but refrained from pursuing them or from turning against Richelieu, his success being judged sufficient to keep the French in check. The Austrians in the meantime had marched into Silesia; Frederick drove them out at Leuten and contented himself with that. After Zorndorf he allowed the beaten Russians to withdraw at their leisure.

Though vigorous in repelling every impending threat, once the danger was past Frederick husbanded his resources, restricting his activity to supporting his Hanoverian or Hessian allies, garrisoning his towns and guarding his frontiers. He made no ambitious plans, undertook no large-scale operations, no devastating attacks or relentless pursuits. To do so would have been inconsistent with his policy, ruinous for his effectives and his budget, and, above all, dangerous in arousing national passions.

Whenever Frederick struck, he made sure that the blow was both necessary and effective, and suited his tactics to the occasion. But the famous oblique order was a skilful adaptation of means to circumstances rather than the panacea which contemporary theorists saw in it. Prussian superiority was no more due to exceptional formations than to the use of superlatively good weapons. Frederick's soldiers were armed in the same way as their opponents: the infantry with musket and bayonet, the cavalry with sabre or lance, while the artillery consisted of light cannon firing between the battalions and a few very heavy pieces which were considered more or less immobile, for the theories of Gribeauval were not yet in fashion. But, on the other hand, Frederick's troops were trained to the last ounce. No other army drilled so much and so well as his. The troops were able to move quickly over various types of country, to deploy rapidly to face in any given direction, to group themselves for volley-fire, to advance without mishaps and, if the need arose, to make an orderly withdrawal.

Monarch and military leader at the same time, Frederick endowed the military art of the eighteenth century with matchless glory. His policy, strategy and tactics, vigorous and moderate at the same time, exploiting circumstances without abusing them, formed a stable and well-knit whole.

But although the King of Prussia had been able to deprive France of her military ascendancy, there was abundant evidence that the eclipse was only temporary. In the early part of the reign of Louis XVI the rehabilitation of the army was undertaken by the Ministers of War, Marshal de Muy and Saint-Germain. Henceforward the regular army was to comprise 112 infantry, 59 cavalry and 8 artillery regiments with complete cadres and effectives, and a nucleus for large formations was formed by 16 territorial divisions. These reforms were carried out against the background of the great intellectual and philosophical movement, which had the Encyclopaedia for both cause and effect, and which showed itself in the army by an intense interest in progressive ideas. It was the time when Guibert published his "Treatise on Tactics" and his "Defence of the Modern System of War", in which he foresaw the organization of the division of all arms, the lightening of packs and supply services, the creation of more flexible formations and the decentralization of command. All these reforms, which were designed to give greater freedom and speed of manœuvre, were later adopted by the Revolution and the Empire. At the same period Marshal de Broglie organized his "Normandy Camp" where troops and staffs, after a surfeit of parades, were made familiar once more with training exercises in various types of country. With the flintlock musket of the 1777 pattern and the paper cartridge, the infantry received an excellent weapon which doubled their fire power. At the same time Gribeauval was carrying out his ideas for making the field artillery stronger in material and more mobile. On the Grand-Master's orders the army adopted the pole-limber, the back sight and elevating screw, the quick-match, which obviated the necessity of pouring the powder into the touch-hole, case-shot, and the cartridge with charge and bullet in one piece. Gribeauval was responsible for the formation of a general reserve comprising 600 cannon of 4, 8, and 12 inches, and 36 6-inch howitzers, making mass artillery bombardment possible, and contributing greatly to future victories. And, finally, fortifications and siege-parks were provided with 8, 12, 16, and 24-inch cannon and 8, 10, 12-inch howitzers such as were possessed by no other state.

In the War of American Independence the French army was to prove its return to pre-eminence. While the seas were dominated by Orvilliers, Estaign, Guichen, Grasse and Suffren, the soldiers of Rochambeau were covering themselves with glory at Yorktown, like those of Bouillé at Saint-Eustace and Crillon at Minorca. In India, on June 13, 1783, the Austrasian Regiment under de Bussy fought the last battle of the *ancien régime* by defeating the English on the Gondelour glacis. In its decline, the monarchy showed renewed strength both in its military power and in its foreign policy. It bequeathed to the nation which it had assembled throughout the centuries all the means whereby it might defend and increase its heritage.

Taking all in all, the work of the *ancien régime* remains efficient and lasting; its strength outweighed its weaknesses, its qualities exceeded its defects. Everywhere the frontiers of France were extended without exhausting the nation: Artois, Flanders, Lorraine, Alsace, the Franche-Comté, Corsica and Roussillon had been incorporated; Belgium and the Rhineland had been opened to French influence; Austria had been humbled and Prussia kept in check; Spain was an ally and Italy friendly; England had been deprived of her enclaves in French territory; France's friends, Scandinavians, Poles and Turks, were sound and faithful; Russia sought her support. France had conquered, lost and partially regained a great colonial empire; Canada was being colonized by Frenchmen; the United States were liberated with the aid of French arms; the king's squadrons cruised off the coasts of Africa. There was no mortgage on the past; the present was guaranteed and provision made for the future.

This edifice was built by the soldiers of the *ancien régime*. When time has borne the men away, leaving their work behind, it is fitting to pay tribute to the workmen.

THE REVOLUTION

I

THE FRENCH REVOLUTION BURST LIKE A BOMBSHELL AMIDST THE EUROPE OF THE *ancien régime*. Its febrile innovations, its boiling passions, its fanatical readiness to shed blood shocked both public opinion and the prudence of governments. Here, it was felt, was no mere rebellion but rather a new order, claiming to impose its subversive influence on ideas, customs and laws.

The movement was serious enough in itself, but, coming from France, it was doubly disturbing. For four centuries France had been an object of jealousy and suspicion for the whole of Europe. Her ambitions were feared and her power envied. Yet Europe was involuntarily imbued with French thought and was to that extent the more disturbed by the path it was taking. Both by hatred and by reason the neighbours of France were driven to take preventive action to make her harmless, even had they not considered her to be in a state of weakness.

An elemental force impelled Europe to go to war. This time it was not a war of interests fought for a province, a local right or a crown, but a war of principles, of whole nations—and correspondingly ferocious. To carry on a war of this nature France had to demand of herself a gigantic and unprecedented effort.

Fundamentally Revolutionary France was in a strong position, with a population in 1789 of twenty-eight millions, equal to the populations of Austria, Prussia and England together. The soil of France was the most fertile in Europe and her workmen the most skilful and hard-working. National unity was an accomplished fact. The peoples on her frontiers—Belgians, Luxemburgers, Palatines, Swiss, Piedmontese—were attached to France by a thousand bonds of ideas, customs, and interests. All these assets were, in time, to be exploited by the dynamism of the Revolution. But the old social framework, containing vast reserves of power, had been shattered with such violence that the result was chaos. The Revolution squandered many of its ample resources and left upon its military effort its own characteristic stamp of greatness and confusion.

At the opening of hostilities with Austria, on April 20, 1792, the army was in a sorry state. There had been no recruiting for the line for two years, the practice being considered as a relic of the disgraceful past. The existing regiments, infected by the general turmoil, were riddled with disaffection. As a matter of fact, everything was done to deprive them of their military virtues. Clubs and societies were allowed to carry on their work with impunity. The traditional regimental names were abolished. Revolts among the soldiers were a constant occurrence and were rarely suppressed. In despair and humiliation the majority of officers—five thousand out of nine thousand—left the country or resigned. Others, either because they had adopted the new ideas or because they felt that the times favoured the ambitious, threw themselves into the movement. Some, with the patience of Job, remained at their posts in silent devotion to their country. At the opening of the States-General Necker declared, "We are not sure of the troops." In January 1790 twenty regiments got rid of their commanders. In December of the same year the Minister de la Tour du Pin denounced before the Assembly "a torrent of military insurrection". At the declaration of war there were 35,000 deserters out of a total force of 170,000 men.

But long before the cannon spoke many politicians and technicians had realized that this numerically reduced army could not bear the heavy load which the Revolution was to place on its shoulders. The monarchy had bequeathed its militia, but its abolition had been demanded in all the *Cahiers* and put into effect by the Constituent Assembly. On paper the National Guard represented a tremendous force of two and a half millions, but its military value was nil. Where, then, should the soldiers come from? The Declaration of the Rights of Man had proclaimed the equality of all Frenchmen; so France would have to be defended by volunteers. In June 1791 the Constituent Assembly resolved to take a contingent of 101,000 men from the National Guard and in the following year the Legislative Assembly asked for an additional 30,000. They were to enlist for one campaign and would be paid at the rate of 15 *sous* a day.

The young men were not displeased to put on their blue uniform. The verdict of the generals was that the elements were good. There remained the task of making soldiers of them. Once the men had been split up into battalions according to their part of the country, they were invited to select their own officers. Whilst certain battalions chose as their leaders ex-officers or n.c.o.s or, at any rate, men of authority, others chose to be led by knaves or fools. The commander of the three departments of Upper Rhine, Upper Saône, and Doubs complained in a letter to the Minister of War that "the method of appointing officers has had the most unfortunate and ridiculous results. The posts have been filled by tricksters, windbags and drunkards." Clothing and equipment, which was the responsibility of the departments, were a knotty problem. As for training the volunteers, if they happened to be near a regular regiment, the latter provided instructors who were "amazed to see so many recruits at the same time, whereas formerly they had received at most eight per year to a company". However, somehow or other they taught them to fall in, to fire and to use a bayonet. If such facilities were not available, the volunteers would receive their training at the same time as their baptism of fire. They arrived in the field full of good intentions, but very uneven in value.

As soon as hostilities began this incoherent mixture of mutinous regulars and partly trained volunteers broke at the first shot. At the sight of the Austrian Hussars the Northern Army under Rochambeau, which was trying to make contact with Coburg in the neighbourhood of Tournai and Mons, was seized with panic. Dillon, who commanded one of the columns, was murdered by his men, while Biron, who led the other, escaped by a hair's-breadth from the blind fury of the fugitives. In the Ardennes Army, despite Lafayette's prestige, the chaos was indescribable. Meanwhile, in the east, the Prussians had crossed almost unopposed into French territory, had taken Longwy and Verdun and were advancing into Champagne.

But the very gravity of the evil imposed its own cure. Despite the storms which raged within it, the country understood that it was lost if those entrusted with its defence shirked their duty. Taking advantage of this trend in public opinion, Dumouriez, Custine, Kellermann and Montesquiou took wise and vigorous action to restore some semblance of discipline. The regulars, ashamed of their plight and far away from their garrisons and ringleaders, recovered their tradition of honour. In the course of active service the volunteers acquired a certain cohesion. Over two thousand inefficient officers were relieved of their commissions. Thanks to the stocks in the northern towns it was possible to replenish equipment and arms. At Valmy the very sight of the revolutionary army was enough to make Brunswick retire. At Jemmapes the enthusiasm of the troops, backed by discipline, made its appearance as a weapon of war. When the Fifth Line Regiment, formerly Navarre, was about to attack Flénu Wood, the colonel, a veteran officer who had served in the regiment for thirty-five years, drew his sword, stood up in his stirrups and gave the regiment's old war cry: "*Navarre! En avant! Navarre sans peur!*" and the soldiers followed suit. The Seventeenth—formerly Auvergne—which was on their right, began to shout in their turn: "*Toujours Auvergne sans tache!*"; whereupon the volunteers, who were coming up behind the regulars, put their hats on the end of their bayonets and filled the air with fervent shouts of "*Vive la Nation!*" The whole body moved forward like one man, and the Austrian position was captured, amidst much shouting, at the first assault.

But as the hardships became greater, this noble enthusiasm waned. For inexperienced troops the winter of 1792–3 in Belgium, in the Treves district and on the Rhine, was a cruel experience. While in Paris the Extremists were at grips with the Girondists amidst the general disorder, the army, thanks to the dishonesty of the various committees and commissars responsible for the administration, was left without the bare necessities of life. The result was plunder, often organized by the officers, who led their men to loot the houses of the wealthy. The Assembly, in theory at least, had abolished the white uniform of the regulars. This provided a further cause for dissatisfaction among the veterans. Pay, which was in the form of *assignats* (the paper money of the

Revolution) was irregular. The troops were inundated by the Extremist clubs with propaganda leaflets and newspapers, such as the *Père Duchêne*, which openly advocated insurrection. Discipline under such conditions collapsed. Wastage through desertion and disease was disquieting, while many of the volunteers of 1791 returned home, claiming that they had enlisted for one campaign and that that campaign was over.

The year 1793 was a black one for France: the bungled offensive in the Low Countries, the defeat at Neerwinden, the treachery of Dumouriez and the loss of Belgium brought discouragement and chaos to a head. On March 25 Valence wrote to the Minister of War: "The disorder and disappointments of the winter, coupled with the lack of officers, have produced among the troops a lack of discipline which is the despair of men who love their country." And this was the moment chosen to declare war on England, the Empire, Spain, and Holland, whose troops were soon to threaten France with deadly peril.

The first need was of men. The army fighting on the frontiers consisted of at most two hundred thousand men whose condition was deplorable. The flow of volunteers had become a trickle; in January and February, of the few hundreds that came to sign on, half were poor wretches in bad health, who were anxious to join the army to get food, and had to be turned away. The voluntary principle had failed to produce the required number of recruits. Henceforward the Revolution was to use compulsion.

In February the Convention, which in the following March was to institute a dictatorship and create the Committee of Public Safety, voted the conscription of 300,000 men. In August it declared all citizens liable to military service, thus constituting a rich reserve of man-power from which the Committee could draw at will. In the year 1793 a million young men were called to the colours.

Their recruitment was no light task. The whole royal system of comptrollers and intendants, with its bureaux, its authority and its experience, had disappeared. Its place had been taken by the Departments which were informed by the Committee of their quota of men. Apart from the obligation of taking bachelors between the ages of twenty and twenty-five before other categories, the departmental authorities were free to adopt their own methods. The usual procedure was to draw lots, but there were cases of more arbitrary practices. Conscription met with a great deal of resistance. Some departments supplied nothing but sickly or criminal recruits. Whole districts rose at the cry of: "Down with the militia!" while recruiting was further impeded by the federalist risings which spread over half the country. But the dreaded commissioners sent into the provinces by the Committee imposed obedience, and soon, willingly or unwillingly, columns of recruits were marching along the roads of France towards the frontiers.

What use was the army to make of this mighty but chaotic flood of recruits? In most cases the conscripts arrived full of the latent enthusiasm and thirst for glory with which, in that amazing period of history, men's minds were dominated. Yet, in the words of Carnot: "The popular frenzy must be organized." At first the Convention had decided to use the new material to create new battalions, but the generals and the commissioners with the armies would have none of it: they had seen enough of these incoherent formations with which the battle area was cluttered. Nor were they willing any longer to tolerate officers chosen at random and despised by their men, officers who had to be cashiered *en masse* after every rout. They recognized the necessity of the greatest possible uniformity in the composition of their armies, with fixed effectives and leaders worthy of the name. "The Republic," wrote Schérer to Bouchotte, the Minister of War, "needs not so much a large number of battalions, as good ones with their full complement of men."

The practice of keeping the new units separate from the line regiments no longer appeared wise. The regulars had an experience and a discipline which the others could scarcely hope to acquire, whereas the volunteers and conscripts brought with them a youthful enthusiasm that the regular officers would have liked to see in their own troops. Moreover, differences in pay, uniform and conditions caused bitterness and jealousy between the two sections of fighting-men. The veterans complained that while they toiled and sweated and bled, all the praise of the Assembly and the Commissioners, all the rewards and promotions went to the newly formed battalions. Not that the prestige of the line regiments suffered by this discrimination. "Every day," said Dubois-Crancé, addressing the Convention, "we find captains and even lieutenant-colonels in the Volunteers asking to be given as a favour the rank of second-lieutenant in a regular regiment." The amalgamation of the professional troops with the citizen levies could no longer be deferred.

In this way the arrival of masses of new recruits on the frontiers led by force of circumstances to the supersession of chaos by order. Henceforward these untrained troops were to be embodied in already existing formations whose experience had given them leaders and cohesion. From sections of the old-established regiments and of volunteers and conscripts, half brigades of three battalions were formed on the model of the regiments of former days. This fusion, which had been demanded from the beginning by the generals, which had been urged by Dubois-Crancé before the Convention in February 1793, and approved by the Assembly in June, became operative towards the end of the year. It produced homogeneous formations, made training easier and provided a regular cadre for the choice and promotion of officers.

From the year 1794 the Revolution had at its disposal the instrument it needed. Since the country had to be saved and the sacred doctrine of the Revolution propagated throughout Europe, France had to have a national army whose power was proportionate to the issues at stake and whose spirit was calculated to lead the people along the path of glory. Conscription was the answer. In the spring of 1794 the Republic had a million soldiers on its frontiers, while its enemies had only half that number. France was the only country to fill her ranks with determined citizens, while Austria used the press-gang, Prussia armed adventurers, England bought mercenaries here, there and everywhere, and Russia used serfs torn from their villages by the whim of local governors. But, more than all that, having abandoned the illusions which had twice wellnigh brought her to disaster, she understood at last that order and discipline are the necessary conditions of power.

Henceforward the armies of the North, of Sambre-et-Meuse, the Moselle, the Rhine, the Alps and the Pyrenees faced their trials with undiminished ardour. "We marched," wrote Marmont in his old age, "surrounded by a kind of radiance whose warmth I can still feel as I did fifty years ago." "We suffered," wrote a grenadier, "but we were proud of our sufferings and tried to laugh at them. Our officers, with their packs on their backs, shared our meagre rations and were mad with joy when they received an overcoat or a pair of boots." Yet these men had to fight at Wattignies, Kaiserlautern, Wissembourg, Fleurus; on the Ourthe, the Roer, the Rhine, at Boulou and Saorgio. Ragged and ill-fed, they endured fatigue, hunger, cold and want in order that the army contractors might increase their profits. But the soldiers had learned not to complain or rebel. The Anglo-Dutch troops, expelled from the Low Countries during the winter of 1794–5, gave themselves up *en masse*, and were amazed to find that their relentless pursuers were "ill-clad ragamuffins". An eye-witness has thus described the astonishment of the burghers of Amsterdam when French troops entered the town on January 20, 1795: "This famous and wealthy city saw the battalions of these valiant fellows, all without shoes or stockings, clothing their nakedness with straw, march through the gates of the town to the sound of music, pile arms and bivouac in the public square amidst ice and snow, and wait without a murmur to be provided with food and lodging." And a volunteer from the

Upper Marne, one Fricasse, wrote a few months later: "We owe our success to our discipline, which kept up our courage when times were bad."

II

After much groping and many mistakes the Revolution succeeded in making a fighting machine of the army which it had forged. The frenzy with which France was torn had long paralysed both the civil government and military command. Even when the Brunswick Manifesto had shown in the clearest possible manner to all concerned the extent of the perils with which the country was faced, the public authorities were in such a chaotic state that they were powerless to play their part in the direction of the war. The disturbed state of public opinion, rebellions and party strife deprived the "Executive Committee" of all tranquillity and of all stability. In the space of twelve months, from the spring of 1792 to that of 1793, there were nine Ministers of War: Duportail, Narbonne, de Grave, Servan, Lazard, d'Abancourt, Pache, Beurnonville, Bouchotte. What is more, not one of them could act without previously consulting the Assembly. All of them allowed events to take their course, concerned much less with the action they proposed to take than with the attitude they should adopt.

Among the generals of the old army, some, like the conscientious veterans Lückner and Rochambeau, heartbroken at seeing themselves prevented from applying their experience to this new form of war, soon ceased to play any part. But others, like Biron, Custine, Kellermann and Montesquiou, showed remarkable resource in most difficult circumstances. Dumouriez excelled in those rarest of gifts: breadth of vision, firmness of purpose, vigour and sureness of touch in execution. Entrusted with the command of the Northern Army after the shameful displays of panic in 1792, he restored order in a matter of days, by means of energy and good sense. Hard-pressed by the Austrians while the Prussians were advancing into the heart of the country, he had the audacity to break off his action with the former in order to attack the latter, and showed in so doing an exceptional gift of freeing himself in unfamiliar circumstances from accepted theories. At Valmy, having made his dispositions for the battle which was to decide the fate of France, he ignored the entreaties of the government, who, horrified at seeing the road to Paris left open, begged him to fall back on Chalons in order to cover the capital. After his victory in Champagne, he did not lose an hour before turning towards the Low Countries until, at Jemmapes, realizing that the strength of his scratch troops resided in their enthusiasm, he made this the basis of his tactics. In the depth of a severe winter, with few or no supplies, he conquered Belgium at one stroke, after which he conceived no less a plan than that of marching into Germany from a previously subdued Holland.

The Revolution had thus inherited from a generous past talented military leaders capable of appreciating at once the type of warfare which the times demanded and possessing in addition the habit of wielding authority. But political passions were to perform the dastardly work of throwing away these advantages. Despite their worth—or rather, on account of it—the generals were deprived by political madness of their prestige, their honour, and, sometimes, of life itself. It was thus with Dumouriez, whose help was sought by the Girondists against the extremists of "The Mountain", and whom the Clubs could never forgive for his popularity. During the whole winter after Jemmapes the Jacobins attacked him relentlessly with insults, threats, and accusations of treason. Not content with this, they undermined his authority among his own troops and even in his own staff. In this they were supported by the delegates of the Minister of War, Pache, if not by the Minister himself. Beneath all the disorders which became more and more frequent among his soldiers, the commander could discern the hand of the politician, against whom he could obtain no redress. Dumouriez, incensed at this mischievous attitude, alarmed at the course the Revolution was taking, and disgusted by the execution of the King, made protest after protest to the Assembly. Between the capital and the general there was a war of abuse and recrimination, which deprived the commander of his peace of mind and of the confidence of his troops. The result was that on the battlefield of Neerwinden, the victor of Valmy and Jemmapes was no longer the man he was. His army fought without conviction; and the left flank, composed of volunteers and "federalists", deserted on the pretext that they were being betrayed. It was then that Dumouriez, forced out of Belgium and incensed at the flood of abuse which his defeat had brought upon his head, lost his sense of duty. He resolved to march on Paris, and negotiated an armistice with the Austrians to this end. When the Convention's commissaries, together with the War Minister, Beurnonville, summoned him to go and explain his conduct before the Assembly—in other words, to offer it his head—he had them arrested and handed over to the enemy. Then, seeing that his troops had lost all desire to follow him, he went over himself to the Austrians.

As soon as the treachery of Dumouriez was known, the Convention set up the Committee of Public Safety, entrusting it with the task, among others, of the conduct of the war. But before the Committee could effectively play its part several months of disorder were to ensue, during which time the country's safety was to depend on the laxity of the enemy and the fortifications of Vauban.

It is true that, in its desire to imbue the armies with the same will to victory with which it was itself animated, the Assembly sent commissioners with unlimited powers to all fronts, with instructions to keep an eye on the generals. The procedure had certain advantages. The presence of the nation's representatives tended to stiffen the resolve of the less determined among the commanders, and to impart to their operations a certain air of ferocity and determination which sometimes impressed a wavering enemy. It often enabled the commander to make his requirements known without delay to the central authority, and in many cases expedited the promotion of officers of value. It was in this sense that commissioners like Carnot and Dubois-Crancé understood their task. Others, however, exploited their position and terrorized the military commanders with the perpetual threat of the guillotine, assuming control of operations without accepting responsibility for them, insisting on the adoption of unworkable plans, and generally aggravating the ills which they claimed to cure.

When Dumouriez's successor with the Northern Army, Dampierre, was killed in an action which he was obliged to undertake against Condé, his troops melted away. Kilmaine, who succeeded him, was dismissed a few days later, to be replaced by Custine, who received orders from the commissioners to pass immediately to the offensive. He refused to obey and paid for his independence with his life. After him Houchard, guilty of having won an incomplete victory at Hondschoote, was sent in his turn to the scaffold. The Army of the North, which in five months, from March to August 1793, had been successively commanded by six generals-in-chief, without counting the temporary appointments, had fallen into a state of complete disorganization. It would have been destroyed, had the English and the Austrians not wasted their time besieging Dunkirk and the fortified towns on the Sambre and Scheldt.

The armies of the East were no better led. The main army, led by Custine, after losing Mainz and falling back under Beauharnais to the Wissembourg lines, saw its general sent to the scaffold and replaced by another one, Landremont. Landremont, forced by the representatives of the government to attack forthwith, was defeated. The same thing happened at Pirmasens with General Moreau. While, after these setbacks, the army was preparing to defend the Wissembourg line, the commissioners again intervened and upset the command. Landremont was replaced first by Curlu and then, soon afterwards, by

Pichegru. The chief-of-staff, Clarke, having been relieved of his post on the morning of the battle, received no substitute. All the divisional commanders saw themselves dismissed or reshuffled at the height of the battle, with the result that the troops, without orders or leaders, gave up their positions, allowing Wurmser to march into Alsace. He was stopped outside Strasburg, less by the French army than by his own quarrels with the Prussians and by his anxiety to besiege Fort Vauban.

In the Alps, General Brunet was sent to the guillotine after his defeat at Reuss. Kellermann, having been found guilty of taking the bulk of his troops into Savoy, whence he had expelled the Piedmontese, instead of pushing on with the siege of Lyons, was cashiered and imprisoned. In the Pyrenees, Generals Servan, Flers, d'Elbecq, Dagobert and Daoust, first of all favoured, and then thrown over by the commissioners, were unable, with the ill-organized and unprovided troops under their command, to prevent the Spaniards from invading the Basque country and Roussillon.

But it was the last straw. In August 1793 Carnot became a member of the Committee, where he was entrusted with military affairs. At long last he was to be enabled to give to the war the direction it so sorely lacked. Not that the Committee was wanting either in determination or in power, even before the arrival of Carnot. But the great merit of the "War Delegate" was to enlighten this hitherto blind resolve and to fructify the powers which, before him, had remained sterile and chaotic.

Amidst the whirlwind by which, all around him, men and parties were being swept away, he concentrated upon his task. "I shut myself up," he wrote, "in the section with which I had been entrusted. I worked sixteen hours a day and listened to nothing that took place outside my office." But then Carnot was an expert—a military engineer who had been studying the problems of war for twenty years. In his capacity of people's representative and commissioner to the armies he had had the opportunity of observing conditions among the troops, of seeing their strength and their weakness, and of forming his own judgment on the personalities of the actual or potential commanders. Carnot surrounded himself with first-rate colleagues: d'Aboville, Galbaud, Laffite-Clavé, Lacuée de Cessac, distinguished officers of the old army and pupils of Guibert and Gribeauval, who formed a competent and homogeneous general staff around the delegate. In this way Carnot brought to the government both skill and experience, thanks to which he snatched victory from chaos.

His first task was to re-establish order in the army. For the whole country he created "assembly camps" where the recruits could receive their preliminary training. On the frontiers he expedited the amalgamation of new recruits and regulars. Above all, imbued with the theories of Guibert and Broglie, he created divisions, made up of various arms, homogeneous and interchangeable, each capable of acting as an autonomous unit. Thanks to this divisional organization, armies which had hitherto been rigid formations found a new flexibility; and the young generals of the Republic, finding themselves suddenly faced with the command of great masses of men, were given a simple and elastic basis for their manœuvres and operations. In the early part of 1795 France had 54 divisions, 260 half-brigades, to bring against the enemy.

All these men had to be provided with arms, munitions, food and clothing, commodities which had to be found in a country rent by disorders which had brought normal life to a standstill; they had to be paid for in a currency which was daily losing its purchasing power, at a time when the country's administrative services had been completely disorganized by the reforms of the Constituent Assembly, decimated by emigration, by prison and the guillotine, and corroded by peculation. The Convention, it is true, applauded Barrère when he described the state of affairs he would like to see realized: "The young men will fight, married men will make weapons; the women will make clothing and tents for the soldiers, the children will make lint from old linen; the old men will be carried on to the public squares to hearten the population." But more effective than this eloquence was the work of Carnot and his fellow-workers. The War Delegate set up a "Commission of Arms, Powder and Mines", composed of officers, scientists and engineers, which, under his direction, undertook the task of supplying armaments. For the equipment, the methods and the skilled craftsmanship for manufacturing weapons cannot be improvised. Fortunately the monarchy had left behind it well-stocked military and naval arsenals in which the Revolution found 730,000 muskets of the 1777 model and more than 2,000 field-pieces designed on the Gribeauval system. The fortified places were equipped with large numbers of 16 and 24 cm. cannon as well as mortars, while the coastal defences were equipped with huge pieces of 36 cm. Carnot did everything in his power to increase the production of armaments. Scientists were called in to help. The discoveries of Monge and Fourcroy in metallurgy made it possible to multiply the production of projectiles by five. Thanks to Berthellot, who invented a method whereby the manufacture of gunpowder was simplified, the ordnance factories increased their output of powder from three to seventeen millions of tons a year. At the same time Chappe, who had been appointed "telegraph engineer", organized a network of rapid communications between the fronts and Paris. On the battlefield of Fleurus, Montgolfier's observation balloons produced enthusiasm among the French troops and alarm among the enemy.

It would appear easier to feed and clothe troops than to provide them with weapons. Carnot, however, was less successful in this field. The supply services, formerly provided in the provinces by royal intendants, and in the field by the commissioners for war, had been abolished. The new departments and war commissioners had to be called upon to replace the missing organizations. But even with the best will in the world the departments showed themselves incompetent; and as for the delegates, those playthings of politics, their efficiency was erratic. For one thing, it was difficult to get an exact estimate of the enormous effectives of the armies and, all the more so, of demands and needs; for the young divisional and corps commanders were loth to concern themselves with administration, to compile detailed reports of stores and equipment. The net result was that the government was forced to rely on contractors, with the safeguard of threatening them with trial before the revolutionary tribunal if they abused their responsibilities. But despite the most severe punishments, the contractors continued to pile up immense fortunes, the root of later corruption under the Directory. In Jourdan's words: "I have had a hundred and fifty thousand men under my command. The government paid scoundrels for a hundred and fifty thousand rations, and the army got ten thousand." Yet, despite all these obstacles, Carnot kept in the field an army of a million fighting-men, and, during the winter of 1794–5, when the troops were fully engaged in enemy country and far from their bases, the hospitals contained "fewer sick soldiers than ever".

III

Victory was to be bought at the price of suffering. Carnot, like Dumouriez before him, had understood that it could be won only by abandoning complicated tactics, formal battles, sieges and picked detachments. These, suitable enough in days when limited objectives were attainable economically and unhurriedly, were ill-adapted to the relentless war of nations. What is more, the procedure of earlier times would have worked to the detriment of the French armies, lacking as they did the training and discipline of their opponents. The right strategy was one whereby masses of troops struck their blows regardless of expenditure and losses, but so hard and so suddenly as to exploit the advantages of numbers and enthusiasm.

This was Carnot's method. When he joined the Committee in August 1793, the northern frontier had been crossed by the enemy, the last strong points on the Scheldt were about to fall, and the road to Paris lay open. He immediately ordered all available reinforcements to the Scheldt in addition to 40,000 men taken, with great daring, from the armies of the Moselle and Rhine. Thanks to these dispositions, Houchard at Hondschotte and, later, Jourdan at Wattignies, found themselves enjoying a considerable numerical superiority over the English and Austrians.

Once the northern invasion had been repulsed, Carnot concentrated his effectives in the east. The right wing of Jourdan's forces was sent to reinforce the Moselle and Rhine armies, which were then able to go over to the offensive. Hoche and Pichegru combined forces to attack the now isolated Austrians who, at Froeschwiller and Wissembourg, could put only 60,000 men in the field against 150,000 Frenchmen. They were defeated and forced to evacuate Alsace. The Prussians, finding themselves uncovered by this retreat, raised the siege of Landau and fell back on Worms.

Having averted the immediate danger, Carnot decided that the moment had come to undertake the conquest of France's natural frontiers. With the enemy encamped at the source of the Oise, Revolutionary France had realized in its turn that no real security was to be found except on the Rhine. In 1794 the northern sector again became the chief theatre of operations. The northern army was strengthened by the addition of 100,000 conscripts who had been enrolled during the winter, and by the entire Army of the Moselle. Pichegru in Flanders and Jourdan in Hainault and the Ardennes had tremendous effectives. At Charleroi and at Fleurus the Regiment of Sambre-et-Meuse fought at an advantage of two to one. Forty thousand French soldiers swept over the Low Countries.

In the east, the situation which had been momentarily endangered by the enemy's advance into the Palatinate was soon restored, the crushing of the revolt in Vendée having allowed Carnot to bring up the victorious troops from Savenay. The French returned to the offensive, pushing back the Austrians from Hohenlohe and the Prussians from Mollendorf. By the end of 1794 French troops were in occupation along the Rhine from Bâle to the sea.

While in the north and east Carnot's strategy of concentrating his forces to ensure numerical superiority saved the country, in the south it restored a very dangerous situation by a co-ordination of effort. At the end of 1793 the most urgent task was to recapture Toulon. By boldly withdrawing troops from the Alps and the Pyrenees Carnot formed a powerful besieging force under Dugommier, which took Toulon in December. Next, doubling the armies of the Var and Eastern Pyrenees by conscript units, he made it possible for Dumerbion to expel the Sardinians from the province of Nice while enabling Dugommier to clear the Roussillon and capture the Camp du Boulu.

Carnot's succesful planning was complemented by the employment of suitable tactics on the battlefield. More by instinct than by reason the armies of the Revolution had adopted a method of fighting which suited their potentialities. The rigid tradition of well-formed ranks and complicated drill movements would have been entirely out of place among those keen, yet ill-trained, troops. In order to fire a shot the infantry soldier had to tear a cartridge with his teeth, pour the powder down the barrel, ram it down with the ramrod, using the casing of the cartridge, push in the bullet against the wad, cock, pour the serpentine powder into the pan and touch-hole, take aim, and fire. In addition to all this he had to clear the clogged barrel at frequent intervals or clean the touch-hole with the priming-needle. Rain, resulting in damp cartridges or a damp lock, caused a misfire. In such conditions it would have been foolish to insist on concerted fire or, for the same reason, on concerted movements by recruits who had been thrown into battle as soon as they had received their weapons.

No such thing was, in fact, demanded of the divisions. They were preceded by a dense swarm of sharpshooters. Each soldier, acting independently, still remained an integral part of the whole. The sharpshooters initiated the attack, profiting by their dispersal to make the best use of cover. The artillery, which had retained its old organization and possessed excellent material, took up its positions and opened fire. Under the covering fire of a hail of bullets and projectiles the main body of the division formed up in columns of great depth but with a narrow front, with the officers at the head of the column. Then, at the right moment, the whole body dashed forward with fixed bayonets, yelling to heighten morale. The crisis did not last long, however, for the range of the muskets was no more than three hundred yards and their rate of fire two shots a minute. If the enemy allowed the attackers to get near, they were usually swept away by the serried masses of the attackers. If not, the attackers retreated, pursued half-heartedly by the much more rigid enemy formations, in order to re-form in the rear.

These were the tatics employed at Wattignies, Wissembourg, and Fleurus, as they had been at Jemmapes. Though simple and expensive, they were vigorous, and well suited not only to numerically strong, enthusiastic troops, but also to the capabilities of the new commanders, who brought to their task great energy, resource and initiative, rather than science, experience and authority. These generals, who led the Republican forces from 1793, had nearly all risen to commander's rank at one bound. Jourdan, who commanded a battalion in 1792, was thirty-two when Fleurus was fought. Pichegru, who started as an n.c.o., was thirty-three at the time of Wissembourg. Marceau, who was a corporal in a line regiment at the beginning of the campaign, commanded a division when he met his death at the age of twenty-seven. Moreau, a former notary's clerk, was commanding an army when he was thirty-three, while Kléber, an architect in peacetime, was thirty-nine when he commanded a division.

Among this galaxy of brilliant young generals Hoche stands out as a symbol. His personality bore all the signs by which his generation was distinguished: a precocious maturity combined with an early development of activity. When he was a frank if turbulent junior subaltern in the French Guards, idle, yet eager for action, he became fired with enthusiasm for the revolutionary movement in which he discerned a chance to satisfy his ambitions. But when he was promoted to the rank of lieutenant in the Army of the Ardennes, he was quick to realize that zeal was impotent without discipline, and from that time onwards he had for both of these qualities the same high regard.

War was to provide him with every opportunity of developing his faculties. During the stormy retreat from Belgium in March 1793 he showed such firmness in the exercise of his humble duties that a great leader singled him out. As captain and aide-de-camp of the former Count Le Veneur, a lieutenant-general in the royal army, who commanded the forces in the Maestricht area, Hoche was the pupil of an experienced soldier. He made useful contacts: Carnot, the delegate to the army of the North, and Couthon, a member of the Committee, both noticed the aide-de-camp who had been entrusted by the general with the task of presenting his reports. And when, in June 1793, Souham needed a second-in-command for the defence of Dunkirk, Hoche was the man chosen for the post. He acquitted himself of his task so successfully that when the siege was over Carnot promoted the young officer to be general-in-chief commanding the Army of the Moselle.

Having attained his exalted rank almost at one bound, Hoche bore his responsibilities soberly and resolutely. His judgment seemed to grow in keenness with the growing complexity of the problems with which he was faced. His men, attracted by the striking discrepancy between his age and his functions, accorded him their unbounded confidence. They bore him no grudge for his failure at Kaiserlautern in an action which exposed him to his full share of danger. Confident that he would restore the situation, they saw him cover himself with glory at Froeschwiller a few days later. At Wissembourg, with 150,000 men under his command, he showed as much wisdom as daring, following his own precept: "Prepare with caution, strike like lightning."

Thus, thanks to the magnitude and speed of events, General Hoche acquired a maturity which in normal times would have crowded the efforts of a long career. Now he had to complete his experience of men; to see envy as a companion to glory; to suffer injustice and adversity. He was not to remain long in ignorance of this lesson. "In my zeal for the Revolution", he was to write, "I thought that it would change the behaviour of mankind. Alas, intrigue is still intrigue!"

His pre-eminence and his success aroused the jealousy of his colleagues, especially of Pichegru, and offended certain members of the Committee, among whom was Saint-Just. The victor of Wissembourg saw himself suddenly transferred to the Army of the Alps, and, once there, arrested and sent under escort to Paris. Thinking that there must be some misunderstanding which he could put right with a word, the general asked to be brought before the Committee. There he found himself face to face with Saint-Just, who, somewhat taken aback despite his usual coolness, showed signs of embarrassment. "Have you a request to make?" he asked. "Yes," replied Hoche, "I demand justice!" Saint-Just, having had time to recover his composure, replied: "You shall have justice, very shortly—the justice you deserve," and Hoche was thrown into prison.

The fall of Robespierre (9 Thermidor) brought about his release. He was now without illusions. Carnot immediately gave him the command of the Army of the Cherbourg Coast, one of the most arduous of missions. In Vendée Hoche was faced with one of those complicated situations in which the instability of the central authority, intrigue at every level and bad faith everywhere combine to tangle the skein. From above he could expect nothing but voluntarily confused instructions, and from below grudging obedience at best. He was surrounded by people who, though ready to take credit for success, refused to share the burden of failure. Yet Hoche made a success even of this task. With no other training than that which he had given himself, the young man found wise solutions for a host of thorny problems, military, political and administrative.

For Hoche had derived from experience both prudence and daring, and his whole bearing bore witness to this happy state of equilibrium. According to one biographer, "matured beyond his age by the habit of command, he relinquished his fiery, sparkling loquence in favour of a cold dignity of bearing and a laconic style of speech". Rouget de Lisle, who saw him at his headquarters a few days before Quiberon, wrote of him: "While he was speaking I was constantly aware of his imposing stature and of his warlike, though modest, bearing. I admired his simplicity, the harmony between gesture and word, between word and tone. Everything in him marked him as an outstanding man."

But while growing in prudence Hoche lost nothing of his daring. A proof of it was his plan for an attack on Ireland. The idea was to transport a French expedition there in secrecy and to promote a rising against England. To convince the Directory of the feasibility of his plan, and to shake the lethargy of the Admiralty, Hoche showed a degree of energy worthy of the great design. But the spectacle of the naval ports with their ships in disrepair and of the indiscipline of the crews at the naval depots convinced the young general that "creative genius" by itself was not enough.

In 1797 Hoche was appointed commander-in-chief of the Army of Sambre-et-Meuse, the most famous army of the Republic. At its head he crossed the Rhine at Neuwied and Düsseldorf, pushed back the Austrians as far as Frankfort and, with Moreau, was just about to bring about their destruction when his victorious advance was halted by the negotiations at Léoben which were to lead to the peace of Campo-Formio. A few months later, as commander of all the forces on the Rhine, he had begun to toy with the idea, so foreign to this loyal-hearted soldier, of political intervention, when death carried off the twenty-nine-year-old generalissimo.

The death of Hoche marked the end of the military age which had witnessed his rise, so that the destiny of the young general seemed one with that of the revolutionary army. This army, born in a surge of enthusiasm, had gradually been obliged by its contact with reality to submit like any other army to the eternal laws which govern all action. It had been obliged to create a hierarchy and to observe discipline. Its apprenticeship was costly both in men, who, fortunately, were numerous, and in energy, a quality of which there was happily no lack. And all the time this struggling army was protected by the remnants, still sound, of the former army, by the fortified places and by the enemy's irresolution. Thereafter, this military machine had sublimated the unchained passions of the time into practical virtues, forging its weapon in the flame of new fires, but in accordance with long established rules, and achieved a monumental work for the good of France. But no sooner had the task been accomplished and the country saved before the army turned its eyes to home affairs. The weakness, the licence and the vices which met its gaze shocked and angered it all the more because its own victories had been won by strength and discipline and honour. Public opinion applauded and invited its power. It only needed some new ambition to pit itself against the anarchy of the state for the well-ranged bayonets of the army to give it enthusiastic support.

NAPOLEON

I

THE ACCESSION OF BONAPARTE WAS WELCOMED BY THE VAST MAJORITY OF PUBLIC opinion. Weary of confusion, France clung to the strong arm which promised to pull her out of it; and by a natural reaction against an excess of disorder and the abuses of liberty, abandoned herself to the master to whom she offered willing obedience. Apart from the irony of certain *salons*, the intrigues of one or two generals and the reserve of a small number of politicians, there was no opposition to the Consul's absolute power.

But this power existed only by virtue of military glory. It concerned itself entirely with war, in which it excelled and in which it found an unbridled career for its activity and its expansion. The nature of the Emperor's power was such that it was bound to drive France into the dreadful cycle of war.

Napoleon found ready for him a splendid army, forged by eight years of campaigning, sure of itself and thirsty for honour, ready for the most ambitious enterprises. Such a perfect instrument in the hands of such a genius can stagger the world by the magnitude of its achievements. But it is a perishable instrument; the rapid succession of campaigns makes its replacement by material of the same quality impossible. Yet in face of this deterioration, the tasks to be performed were to grow proportionately greater. At first Europe, weakened and divided, could offer only an unco-ordinated resistance, but its strength was to increase with its reverses. At the same time every victory only whetted Napoleon's appetite, magnifying his plans beyond the bounds of the possible, until the day came when the relationship of ends and means collapsed, and with it all the vainly constructed plans of genius.

The Directory bequeathed to the First Consul a new system of recruiting, both simple and categorical enough to be applied without difficulty by a zealous administration, and extensive enough to allow the impatient energy of the master to bleed France of her youth without infringing the law or creating unpleasantness in the legislative assembly. A few months before Brumaire (November 1799) Jourdan got the "Five Hundred" and the "Ancients" to pass a conscription bill which regularized the revolutionary "requisition". Henceforward all unmarried men between the ages of twenty and twenty-five became liable to active military service for a period of four years, beginning with the youngest classes. The draft had to be voted by the representatives of the nation and chosen by lot. In the minds of the legislators conscription would enable the army to be kept up to strength by a moderate call-up, and in the early days the First Consul made use of the institution without abusing it. Up to the year 1802 he asked for no more than some 30,000 men a year. He took good care, however, not to demobilize the old soldiers. Nor was this regular call-up immediately effective; out of 63,000 conscripts raised with great difficulty in 1801 and 1802, only 49,000 ever reached their units.

But for the series of wars which opened with the rupture of the Peace of Amiens, and for plans which grew bolder with success, Napoleon needed men. He needed men to threaten England at the Camp of Boulogne, to cross the Rhine, to expel the Austrians from Southern Germany, to march into Vienna and to conquer two emperors at Austerlitz. He needed men to occupy Italy, to seize the Illyrian provinces, as well as to guard Vendée and the coasts. He needed men to crush Prussia, to keep his hold on Northern Germany and to try out the Continental Blockade. He needed men for his Polish campaign, by which he sought to revive Poland and persuade Alexander of the futility of fighting against France. No wonder that his demands were constantly increasing; 60,000 men in 1803, 65,000 in 1804. In the following year the Senate assumed the right of voting the annual contingent, a right reserved up to that time to the Legislative Body. Thus the last traces of opposition faded away. The Emperor secured a grant of 80,000 men on account of the 1805 class and another 100,000 on the previous years. But no sooner had these men joined their regiments before Napoleon, from Moravia, asked for a further 80,000 in advance from the next call-up. In December 1806, by a decree of the Senate, he was granted 80,000 from the 1807 class and, in April 1807, another 80,000 from the 1808 class.

Despite the glory of the Empire, conscription met with considerable resistance. For centuries the French people had borne only the lightest military burdens, and no foreign invader now threatened the soil of their country. There was, therefore, no enthusiasm for Napoleon's demands. "A conscript is a lost child", was a common saying among the people; and although the Government endeavoured to spare the departments in the west, south-west and south, still muttering with memories of the Chouans and Federalists, although it dealt gently with the big towns out of respect for their rebellious leanings, although substitutes were permitted, making it possible for middle-class parents to "buy a man" for their son, a tremendous effort was required to collect and despatch the prescribed contingents. This task fell to the prefects, goaded on by the central government. In a letter to these officials Fouché wrote: "A prefect who fails to make conscription work cannot deserve the confidence of the Emperor"; while the Emperor expressed the following view of the duties of prefects, taking care that his words should come to the ears of the people concerned: "My opinion of their zeal and of their services depends on the success of conscription." Nor did the government neglect the collaboration of the clergy: "The spirit of the shepherd is judged by the conduct of his sheep," the bishops were told. A whole system of repression was put into force against those who resisted; their villages had to provide substitutes and pay fines; gendarmes were billeted on their families, man-hunts were organized to track them down.

Despite the very great numbers of men liable to be called up, a considerable selection was possible up to the year 1807. A hundred thousand men per annum taken from a class of double that number was by no means beyond the powers of a country which had reached its natural frontiers and whose fertility, already high in pre-Revolution days, now provided large numbers of conscripts for the Emperor. The recruiting authorities were able to pick and choose, to reject the sickly or the undersized and to reserve those who were not yet sufficiently developed. Those who joined the colours were robust young men, mostly peasants, used to hard living, to long journeys and heavy burdens. They were gloomy at first, as they had every cause to be—"I cried my eyes out," said Coignet, "and my leave-taking was sad"—but they were soon converted by the all-absorbing roughness of their new life. Even on the long march to their depots the incidents of the journey, the strangeness of their billets, began the uprooting process. Once with their regiment everything combined to carry it a stage further; even the most second-rate conscript could feel the warlike ardour with which the Grande Armée was inspired. The regiments contained, of course, a considerable number of old soldiers, toughened by the ups and downs of many campaigns, steady under fire, grousing and quarrelsome and not easily amenable to discipline.

It is no matter for surprise that, in the army of the Empire, where the old soldier set the tone, mere differences of rank were incapable of sustaining discipline. These men, whose whole training had been received in the field, who had been constantly on the march or in action, were too good judges of men and situations to put their trust in any and every commander. The junior officers had little more authority than that which accrued to them from their courage. Most of them had risen from the ranks by force of circumstances and, though able to read, differed neither in manner nor education from their fellows. If they showed courage and presence of mind, their men would follow them into battle; but each man obeyed only his immediate superior. The higher ranks were of very recent growth, and owed any authority they possessed to their own capacity. Rank counted for nothing; everyone knew that promotion was largely a matter of luck. At Marengo the general of a division, Chambarlhac, showed signs of cowardice; on the following day his men greeted him with hoots and shots. He forthwith disappeared and was never heard of again.

Napoleon, however, did much to raise the intellectual and social level of his officers. This was no easy task, for not only did the middle classes buy their sons out of the army, but the former military aristocracy had been decimated by emigration and the scaffold. The Emperor founded schools like Fontainebleau, Saint-Cyr, Metz, and Châlons, entrance to which was, in theory, competitive, but to which in fact he sent carefully selected young men. He created a corps of volunteers of good family, which he called "Velites of the Guard", and intended to serve as a nursery for future subalterns. He welcomed any émigré officers who offered their services. On the other hand, when by chance he found the necessary leisure—during the Peace of Amiens, for example— he pensioned off those officers who were exhausted or inefficient. But despite all these efforts the quality of recruits was not materially improved. The pupils from the schools, who left too young and without sufficient training (so great was the haste to fill the vacant places and to provide cadres for new formations), lacked the necessary authority over their men. The Velites were slaughtered in large numbers during every campaign, while many of the returned émigrés sought a quiet life and ensconced themselves in offices well behind the lines. So the average quality of officers and the relationship between commanders and their men did not change, while obedience remained very relative. Something else was needed to sustain the army during the exacting trials into which it was to be launched.

Napoleon set out to supply the missing element. To carry with him a generation whose minds had been saturated with the epic deeds and fiery passions of the Revolution, he turned to the spirit of emulation, of honour, to the desire for personal glory. He placed the stamp of his own greatness on everything. Feeling that his own genius supplied the motive force for these masses of fighting men, he identified every ambition, every distinction, and every reward with his own person and his own prestige. It was as if the army were for ever engaged in a competition organized and judged by the Emperor, with glory as the prize.

With this purpose in mind he created crack regiments in whose privileged ranks every soldier was eager to serve. He took the cream of his regiments to form the Guards. No one was eligible who had not done four campaigns or been wounded twice or distinguished himself by some outstanding feat. In the Guards every soldier had the rank and the pay of a sergeant, every corporal those of sergeant-major and every sergeant-major those of second lieutenant. The Emperor's escort was always formed by the Guards. The Guards had the best barracks and the best camps; they marched by the shortest route and received extra rations. A soldier would do anything to become a grenadier, a sharpshooter, a cavalryman, or a bombardier in the Guards. If he was unsuccessful and obliged to remain with his own regiment, he could nevertheless win precious distinctions: a stripe for five years' service (some men wore as many as six) gave a man the right to higher pay and put the "old sweat" in the front rank, in front of the conscripts—at the head too, of the attacking column, but also well in view of the Emperor at a review or a march past. A man who distinguished himself by an exceptional deed of valour received a weapon of honour—a musket, sword or lance—with silver embellishments, which the soldier was proud to bear and which brought with it double pay in addition to a gratuity. And above all these distinctions was the Cross, that dazzling token of merit, the symbol of an exclusive, privileged caste, by which the humblest became a knight. Napoleon distributed it widely, though not prodigally, and "ceremoniously conferred it upon the private soldier on the same day and with the same gestures as upon a Marshal of the Empire or the Grand Chancellor".

At the same time as he stimulated emulation by these methods the leader gave many proofs of his concern for and care of those who were ready to lay down their lives for his glory. He knew how to speak to them, carefully, calculating every gesture, how to impress them by the pomp of his surroundings and to touch them by his simplicity. When he reviewed a garrison, which he did frequently and with the greatest care, he would interview several of the men whose names he pretended to know, gave orders that the petitions which the men stuck on the end of their ramrods should be collected, and invited any soldiers who had anything to say to step forward. Then he would give orders for the distribution of wine or brandy. One day he put into orders that he was giving the grenadiers a cap, which they henceforward wore with pride—though it differed not at all from the one they were already wearing—because it was now the Emperor's Cap. He never lost an occasion of associating his soldiers with his greatness. Often he would invite them to dine with him. On his coronation day he filled Notre Dame with them. Victorious troops returning to France were received by the municipal authorities. Banquets, like the one given by Paris to the Guards in 1807, were given in their honour, and the doors of the theatres were thrown open to them. On the occasion of the birth of the King of Rome every soldier received a present.

In the course of a campaign Napoleon would show himself everywhere; he would spend hours visiting outposts, bivouacs and artillery parks, but always unexpectedly, so as to give the impression that he was everywhere and that nothing could escape him. After the battle he would inspect the battlefield, salute the troops, enquire about the wounded and reward instantaneously and in the most dramatic manner soldiers who were pointed out to him. Morvan in his *Soldier of the Empire* has described the leader on the evening of Abensberg as he inspected General Legrand's division. "Which regiment has suffered most, General?" "The Twenty-sixth Light." He goes to it. "Introduce the bravest of your officers, Colonel." Lieutenant Guyot is sent for. "I make you a baron and I grant you an annuity of four thousand francs. Which is the bravest private?" A battalion commander pushes forward a grenadier called Bayonet. "I name you a knight of the Legion of Honour and here is a certificate entitling you to one thousand five hundred francs a year." The Emperor departs, leaving the regiment stunned with emotion.

Napoleon saw to it that the general public was made aware of the army's glory. To this end he organized, especially in Paris, sparkling military parades which dazzled the soldiers almost as much as the sightseers. On the Champ de Mars or on the Place du Carrousel he paraded the garrison troops in their handsome uniforms. First came the infantry of the line with the French blue coats over white tunics and breeches, black gaiters and three-cornered hats, preceded by their grenadiers, imposingly tall in their bearskin caps. Then the light infantry in dark blue coats with light yellow facings; next the artillery in black. Then the cavalry; the carabineers with the red silk on their helmets, the cuirassiers in their coats of red and gold, dragoons in blue, chasseurs in green, hussars with tuft and sabretache, wearing their frogged cloak hanging from the shoulder. And, last of all, the Guards. "The grenadiers in blue coats with white facings, white dimity jackets, white breeches and gaiters, silver buckles at the knees and on their shoes, powdered hair with a six-inch pigtail and, on top of everything, the huge bearskin with its big red cockade and its brass medallion on which the gilt eagle spreads its wings." Leading their amazing band which, according to a contemporary account, included thirty negroes, and in which the sound of the flute pierced the clash of the brass and the roll of the drums, marched the drum-major, "nine foot high including everything" and gilt all over—his outfit cost thirty thousand francs—and surmounted by an extraordinary plumed hat on which, into the bargain, waved a tremendous feather. After the grenadiers came the chasseurs, in green; the artillery, in black; and the sappers with their scarlet-trimmed helmets. The cavalry brought up the rear: grenadiers in blue and gold coats, bearskins with red plumes, chasseurs in green coats frogged with gold, with red and white cloaks, dragoons with blue tufted helmets and, last of all, "the mamelukes, strange with their turbans, short Turkish coats, red trousers, mounted on Arab horses, which take fright and prance at the sound of the kettledrums".

But all this magnificence was nothing but a façade which, once the army was in the field, made way for a revelation of the wretched plight of the soldiers. Napoleon set out to ennoble even their wretchedness. The widows and children of soldiers killed in action became entitled to a pension. In point of fact the cost of this measure was not high, as few of the conscripts were married men. The Emperor granted a pension of two hundred francs after Austerlitz and of five hundred after Wagram to the families of the fallen, and adopted their children. "The boys," he wrote, "will be educated at my expense at Rambouillet and the girls at Saint-Germain." He restored the institution of the Invalides, which had been neglected by the Revolution, and made a large grant to the pensioners whom he reinstalled in their hospital, founding branches at Louvain and Avignon. He put at their disposal the Palace of Versailles, where many of them were lodged, and placed at their head a great leader, Marshal Sérurier. Men who had remained fairly active were found employment or were grouped into companies of veterans in one or another of the fortified towns where they could perform duties as guards or instructors. Those who had lost their sight or one of their limbs were made lieutenants and recommended by Napoleon to his relatives. To the young Vice-Queen of Italy he wrote: "Let your purse be always at their disposal. Nothing could be closer to my heart". He visited the Pensioners, tasted their soup and offered them snuff. He made many a delicate gesture on their behalf, as, for example, when on entering Berlin after Jena, he sent the sword of Frederick the Great to the survivors of Rosbach.

In this way Napoleon sustained the moral strength of his soldiers by the breath of his own body. Everything—honour, discipline, rewards and even justice—flowed from him, returned to him, shone with his glory. Duty and ambition, work and merit, depending on his word alone, had no other object than to give him satisfaction. Every man's mind was concerned with him: "Is he pleased? Is he dissatisfied?" Those were the great questions discussed at every level throughout the army. A company fought twice as well when it fought under his eyes. The wounded on the battlefield saluted him, and the dying rallied to acclaim him. All the enthusiasm in men's souls expressed itself in one formula: "Long live the Emperor!"

He inspired the talents of his senior commanders quite as much as the devotion of the lowly. Napoleon's Marshals, however brilliant, could be nothing but his executants to whom the exclusive and imperious genius of the master left but little initiative. Those who aroused his mistrust or jealousy were denied a command. Of the great generals of the Republic, Hoche, Kléber, Championne, Desaix were dead; Moreau and Pichegru had ruled themselves out by intriguing or plotting. But Jourdan, Kellermann, Brune, Pérignon, Sérurier, Moncey, who were appointed Marshals, performed nothing but administrative or honorific duties. Lecourbe, of whom Napoleon nevertheless said that "he is very brave and a better man than Ney", remained without an appointment. Macdonald, a friend of Moreau, whom he dared to defend, remained in disgrace for a long period. Even Masséna, who, according to the Emperor, "possesses military qualities before which one should kneel", was kept in the background until 1809. On the other hand, the Emperor made use of that unbending warrior Davout, the most competent of the soldiers in his service. Davout was the type of shortsighted man who insists on seeing everything for himself, the prudent man who knows when to be bold, capable of planning as well as executing commands. Napoleon usually gave him an independent role, which kept him clear of the Emperor's immediate circle. The Marshal, for his part, despite a certain gruffness and awkwardness, knew how to give way. Napoleon never hesitated to eclipse his subordinate's fame when he considered it untimely; in his bulletin on the battle of Jena he scarcely mentioned Auerstadt.

His usual lieutenants, however brilliant when under his orders, however skilful under his guidance, however indefatigable under a master who knew no rest, lost much of their value when they found themselves in a situation which called for individual action. But in his hands they formed an admirable executive instrument. Berthier, the ideal chief-of-staff for Napoleon, was a tireless worker with a supple brain, quick to seize and translate his master's wishes into orders, knowing everybody and what should be said or written to each individual, thoroughly conversant with all the inner mechanism of the army, a master of liaison work, and perfectly at home with reports, returns and registers. Murat, of whom it was said that he had not his equal in the cavalry, was the man for feats of daring rather than for cool calculations, unsuited to command large-scale operations but a first-rate man for dashing charges and hell-for-leather pursuits. "Without me," said the Emperor, "he is nothing; at my side, he is my right arm." Ney, erratic in everything except courage, sometimes showed the greatest shrewdness, and at others an obvious failure to understand. Endowed with energy which, according to the occasion, became admirable perseverance or unfortunate obstinacy, heroic and impulsive, carried by his temperament to the height of success or the depths of failure, he was variously held by Napoleon to be "worth two hundred millions" and "mad". Lannes, "a pygmy when I took him and a giant when I lost him", was a man whose mind improved with his rank, "better than any of the generals when it is a case of manœuvring twenty-five thousand infantry"; a man who "did not understand large-scale tactics but might, perhaps, have learned". Soult, a remarkably able tactician but no strategist, was one of the most distinguished generals of second rank, an organizer rather than a creator. Marmont, the artillery expert of this brilliant group, an educated and cultured man with a quick and supple brain, though his character hardly matched his intelligence, was a special favourite of the Emperor, who declared that he "loved him like a son". With Bernadotte, whose ambition knew no bounds and who was as skilful in war as in everything else, military talent was often inhibited by personal interests. Among the other Marshals were: Augereau, brutal, brave and dashing, but lacking in judgment and dazzled by his own fortune, Lefebvre, Victor, Bessières, experienced and valiant soldiers.

These military leaders were ambitious men, and everything conspired to encourage their ambition. Seeing that a soldier like themselves had succeeded in climbing on to the throne of the world's most powerful monarchy, that the Revolution had torn down the traditional barriers which set bounds to opportunity, and that in the convulsion which had shaken Europe there were empty thrones, provinces for sale to the highest bidder, and wealth for those who were strong enough to lay hands on it, they were ready to wage war and accept risks in the hope of making their fortunes. The Emperor did everything in his power to encourage them. He created a new nobility. He made kings of Bernadotte and Murat. He married Berthier to the daughter of the King of Bavaria and allowed Marmont to play at kingship in Illyria, Davout to hope for the Polish throne, Junot to dream of the sceptre of the Braganzas, and Soult to rule in Andalusia with the powers of an absolute monarch. He doled out to them immense fortunes, gifts of money, baronial domains, fiefs in conquered territory, representing incomes of millions of francs. Thus these obscure officers who, under the monarchy, would have finished as subalterns and dreamed of nothing better to end their days than as pensioners at the Invalides or as porters at the Palais Royal—these sons of coopers, tanners and vine-growers were loaded by the Emperor with wealth and honours at an age at which they were able fully to enjoy these satisfactions.

For these men were young. At the time of the Camp of Boulogne Marmont was 30, Murat 33, Davout 34, Ney, Lannes, Soult 35, Mortier and Bessières 36, Oudinot 37, Victor 38, and Macdonald 39. They found idleness irksome, but revelled in action. Blessed with iron constitutions, they gladly suffered the fatigues of campaigning, endured cold, heat and rain; they could remain in the saddle for days together, go without sleep and eat anything. In the art of war they were already experienced veterans. Moreover, Napoleon was always there to make the general plan; all he asked of them was to perform the particular task at which each of them excelled. Their contribution consisted of an instinctive grasp of the immediate situation, daring interventions, and the exercise of their personal influence over their troops.

What were the elements of which the Imperial Army was formed? Carefully selected conscripts whom no family ties or personal interests withheld from sacrifice; tried veterans of twenty fights, men who had seen much and suffered much; junior officers whose only authority sprang from their courage and their services; in the higher ranks, young officers who were burning to distinguish themselves; ambitious senior commanders, conscious that their own careers were bound up with that of their master—such were the elements of the Grande Armée which Napoleon found ready to his hand, and which he inspired with devotion to himself and led towards the glittering mirage of glory.

An army like this in the hands of a leader like Napoleon was bound to smash the enemy forces. What effective resistance could there be from the Austrians of 1805 who recruited their troops by the system in vogue under the *ancien régime*, mixing in the same unit men from fifteen different races, sickened with parades and pettifogging details, lined up to the accompaniment of "blows from the sticks of the mechanical drill-sergeants", led "by old, slow, lazy, stubborn captains", and organized from far away by the regulations and orders of a crowd of pretentious clerks tucked away in their offices? How could anything be expected from a monarchy that put its regiments under the command of noble lords acting as improvised colonels, and its armies under generals whose military ideal was to offend nobody and who were themselves held on the end of a string by pompous Aulic Councils? What could the Russians do—poor dazed serfs, rounded up by their local governors, trained by kicks from the boots of their n.c.o.s and catechized by their popes? Disciplined, yes, but passive, ready to die rather than to fight, strong by their fatalistic self-sacrifice in defence, but clumsy in manœuvre, dying of starvation in hundreds while their commissariat officers filled their own pockets. What could the Prussian army do—petrified in its glorious routine, with mercenary soldiers, still drawn up in close formation, stiff in their long coats, weighed down by their packs, choked by their collars, cramped by a mass of straps, braces and belts, marching without enthusiasm or confidence behind fifty-year-old captains, colonels of sixty, and septuagenarian generals? Decimated by sickness before the battle, the Prussian army spent the night before Jena shivering with fear, while men fainted with hunger and cold, lacking shelters which they did not know how to build and fires which they dared not light. For this army defeat immediately became a rout. When the fugitives were stopped at Magdebourg their shattered morale received the heartening ministrations of "Governor Kleist, a decrepit old man smothered in decorations, who reviewed the troops, tottering along the line, bent and leaning heavily on his stick".

The state of affairs in the *Grande Armée* provided a striking contrast. Once the Emperor had selected the most favourable place and time to strike, had fixed his dispositions, chosen his terrain and decided the methods by which it could be exploited, the troops were capable of providing that speed of manœuvre and that irresistible punch in battle which carried all before them. Napoleon's dispositions in face of divided and ill-prepared adversaries proved in practice their deadly efficiency. In a few days the French army was able to surprise an enemy who thought he was at a safe distance; a single battle sealed the destiny of a state. Napoleon struck so swiftly and so hard that allies had no time to confer and neutrals no desire to intervene. Scarcely had Austria, in 1802, threatened the Emperor before, to her horror, she saw him march into Southern Germany, exterminate the army which she was holding ready in that country, and march upon Vienna. When Prussia was thinking of joining the Austrians and Russians, her ambassador who came post-haste with an ultimatum to Napoleon's headquarters arrived just in time to congratulate him on the victory of Austerlitz. In 1806 the Prussians were totally defeated on the Saale while the Russians were still a hundred leagues away. In the following year the Russians were defeated in their turn before the desperate and defeated coalition could re-form round them.

For the *Grande Armée* could cover a hundred and forty leagues in twenty days, as they did from Boulogne to Ulm, followed by a hundred and fifty more in less than a month, from Ulm to Brünn. They marched without supplies, living on what they could carry in their haversacks or find on the road. They bivouacked wherever they stopped, rolled in their greatcoats near the camp-fire, or, if the weather was too bad, in huts made of branches and straw. The length of the day's march, the discomfort of the halts and the irregularity of the rations strung out the columns, which, followed as they were by considerable numbers of stragglers and marauders, gave the impression of "advancing in disorder" and greatly astonished an enemy accustomed to keep its ranks and files during the march. The disorder was more apparent than real, for the soldiers who "dodged the column" in order to find some dinner for their squad soon caught up with their comrades again. At the first sound of the cannon the units were at full strength.

Under the cover of their advance guard, of the flanking units of cavalry and of outposts who engage the enemy's fire, the divisions are massing. The commanders make their reconnaissance, the troops get ready, prepare their weapons, eat if possible and drink a tot of brandy handed round by the *cantinières*. The impassibility of the old soldiers is a powerful aid to the moral of the conscripts. An air of cheerfulness is *de rigueur* before the battle. Often the Emperor tours the battlefield, gives orders, says a few words of encouragement which are immediately passed on. Sometimes, as at Austerlitz, Jena, Eylau, and Friedland, darkness falls before all these preliminaries are completed. During the night there is a lull in the firing. It is a sleepless night, spent in counting the number of camp-fires on the enemy's side. Some of the more enterprising scour the neighbouring villages for food; others conceal their nervousness beneath a forced facetiousness.

The great battle is joined at first light. The artillery opens up with a terrific bombardment that makes the earth tremble, deafens the troops and spreads a pall of smoke over the ground. At first the four- to twelve-pounders do little damage, for the opposing bodies of infantry are still far away. The projectiles plough up the soil and make gaps in ranks which are soon closed up again. "Keep your heads up!" yells the *serre-file* from the rear, and the soldiers try valiantly not to "bow to the bullet". A compact line of musketeers—usually the *voltigeurs*—opens fire, while the units who are to make the attack form up in columns with the grenadiers in the front ranks. Then at the appointed moment the men fix bayonets, the officers place themselves at the head of their troops with a sword in one hand and a pistol in the other; the standard is raised in the centre, the band strikes up an inspiring tune—"*On va leur percer le flanc!*" "*La victorie est à nous!*" or "*Fanfan la tulipe*"; the drums beat a wild tattoo, and the infantry moves forward with weapons at the ready.

The defenders have deployed their leading battalions in order to bring to bear a maximum of fire-power. But since their range is little more than three hundred yards and their rate of fire at most two shots a minute, they are powerless to stop a determined attacker. The latter, advancing in columns against an enemy drawn out in a long line, has every chance of breaking through, only to be exposed in his turn to the counter-attack which, for the same reason, often succeeds in hurling him back. He re-forms and, strengthened by reinforcements, returns to the attack. This alternation of attack and counter-attack makes the infantry engagements particularly fierce. Certain positions change hands several times within a few hours: Castel-Ceriolo at Marengo, for example, Vierzehnheiligen at Jena, the cemetery at Eylau, the wood and hamlet of Sortlack at Friedland, or the villages of Essling and Aspern at Essling and Wagram.

Once the ranks are broken, however, whether advancing or retreating, the enemy cavalry loses no time in making a charge. If the infantry have time and presence of mind enough to form a square, they suffer no great harm and can watch the flood of horsemen helplessly milling round them. If not, they will be sabred and scattered unless their own cavalry squadrons arrive quickly enough to rescue them.

Thus the battle of attrition takes its course, using up effectives and wearing down morale. The Emperor calmly watches the battle, usually remaining motionless at an observation point where messages can reach him easily, sitting or lying on the ground when he can spread out his maps, sheltering in some hovel when obliged to take cover from rain or snow, quietly giving orders to his liaison officers and listening to their reports without making interruptions. For though usually abrupt and unceremonious, while a battle is in progress he is gentle and considerate with everyone, "especially when things are going badly".

At length the situation for which he has been waiting has matured. The balance between the two sides, both engaged to the full, is delicate. It can be upset in a matter of minutes by hitting the enemy hard and suddenly on his sensitive spot. Napoleon's genius excelled in bringing about such a situation, in procuring the means of dealing with it and in recognizing the right moment and the suitable action to be taken. For this task he used his infantry reserve, supported by the general artillery reserve, and followed by the heavy cavalry whose onslaught clinched the success of the operation. Austerlitz provides an example of the method; the attack on the plateau of Pratzen by Soult, Bernadotte, the Guards, and Oudinot's grenadiers smashed the enemy's centre, while the stubborn resistance of Lannes on the left, in the neighbourhood of the Santon, and of Davout on the right, on the Goldbach, paved the way for the decisive blow. At Jena, the offensive of Lannes, Augereau and Soult between the Mühlthal and the Löbstedt ravine wore down the Prussians before they were routed by Ney's sudden and concentrated attack. It was Ney again who, at Friedland, supported by the two hundred guns of Sénarmont, ensured victory during the afternoon by capturing the bridges over the Alle after Lannes, Mortier, and Grouchy had been struggling with the Russians for the possession of ground since three o'clock in the morning.

To ensure, moreover, that the final effort should be as vigorous as possible, the Emperor would intervene in person. He would appear on horseback at a prearranged spot, watch the columns massing for the attack, ride along the artillery line and question generals and corps commanders. When the veterans saw him, they knew that the great moment had come. He took up his position at a point from which he could observe the operations without delay or intermediary. This often happened to be under fire, close to the batteries. As soon as events allowed, he would move forward towards the enemy, and allow the fact to be known. From one end of the battlefield to the other the word went round that the Emperor had moved forward. Men took fresh courage just in time to give added dash to the general offensive which was then imminent, and the final stages of the battle reached the pitch of intensity which favoured its full exploitation.

II

Despite the prodigious successes which his genius wrung from the army under his command, up to Tilsit the Emperor took care never to assume a task which was beyond his means. However ambitious and overbearing his policy had been in the period from 1805 to 1807, it had preserved a character of relative moderation. If Napoleon plundered his victims, there was at least the excuse that they had attacked him. If he kept the whole of Italy, he could maintain that since the House of Savoy, the Venetian Senate, the Princes of the North and the Bourbons in Naples had always been hostile to France, their expulsion was a measure of self-defence. True, he had founded the Confederation of the Rhine, strengthened Bavaria at the expense of Austria, from whom he had wrested her provinces on the Adriatic, but was it not necessary to weight the scales in Germany against those hostile states, to reward one's friends and to cut off the Hapsburgs as far as possible from the sea and from English influence? If he dismembered and humiliated Prussia, retained possession of Hanover, fashioned a greater Westphalia and clung to Magdeburg, it was because he had nothing but hatred and treachery to expect from the Hohenzollerns. He had given a body to the soul of Poland, had encouraged Swedish designs on Finland, striven to restore Turkey and to conciliate Persia. But while mollifying Alexander it was surely prudent to keep him in check in the west and in the north; for why, in order to please Russia, should Napoleon give up the idea of the road to the east along which he might one day strike a blow at that irreconcilable enemy, England?

After Tilsit, however, at the very moment when his army was no longer the perfect instrument it had been, the Emperor's political plans lost all touch with reality. His victories, decisive as they were, had not been won without losses; 35,000 men had been killed in the period from the Camp of Boulogne to Friedland. The wounded totalled 150,000, half of whom would never be fit for service again, for despite the efforts of Larrey, the field hospital service was extremely primitive and surgeons knew no method of preventing gangrene apart from amputation. In addition, 100,000 men had died of disease or exhaustion in the hospitals of the Rhineland or on the roads of Germany.

The wastage was all the more serious because from this time onwards the enemy was able to put into the field ever-increasing forces, inspired more and more by national feeling. Hofer's Tyrolese had already shown in 1809 what an exasperated nation could do. Spain was to provide the Emperor with a cruel confirmation of the same lesson. England, having decided to make a serious military effort, sent to the Peninsula first-rate troops who showed their toughness in their first encounters with Napoleon's soldiers. At Talavera the corps under Victor was surprised and decimated by the English fire. "Never had such running fire been heard before," said one witness. In 1809 Austria put a very different army in the field from any that had gone before. It was carefully recruited, and commanded by the Archduke Charles, who ranked high enough both in respect of generalship and birth to make himself independent of a tyrannous court. The Russia of 1812, roused by what she held to be a sacrilegious invasion, drew from her population masses of resolute fighters. Prussia, despite treaties which attempted to reduce her armed forces to 40,000 soldiers, raised an army of 80,000 in 1813 and later, after Pleisswitz, 150,000—not well trained, perhaps, but filled with enthusiasm and hatred. Inspired by Prussia's example the whole of Germany armed vast numbers of young men. In 1814 France was invaded by a million enemy troops, while another million were preparing to follow them. These masses were commanded by generals schooled by reverses. The tenacious Duke of Wellington, the indomitable Blücher, and the methodical Schwartzenberg, to whom must be added Bernadotte, were leaders of quite another stamp from that of their predecessors Mélas, Mack, or Brunswick.

Every year, moreover, conscription weighed more heavily on France. In January 1808, computing the cost in effectives likely to be incurred in Spain, the Emperor asked for 80,000 men from the 1809 class, and then, in the August after Baylen, with an eye on Austria's armaments, for 80,000 more from the earlier classes in addition to a further 80,000 from the 1810 call-up. These drafts provided the soldiers for Eckmühl, Essling and Wagram. A further 36,000 recruits were called up in September 1809. The year of peace—1810—was the glorious year of victory, the year of the Emperor's marriage. There was to be no conscription! This did not prevent 40,000 boys of 16, 17 and 18 from being taken for the navy, or 10,000 French subjects from the new departments, freed from Austrian military service, from being enlisted. What is more, profiting by the lull in foreign wars, the government was able to track down 50,000 deserters, and to lick them into shape at Belle-Isle, Ré, or Walcheren before sending them to join their regiments.

But the war which Napoleon was anxious to wage against the Tsar without abandoning either the Spanish or Italian campaigns and without any relaxation, to say the least, of the Continental Blockade, made yet greater demands on manpower. The year 1811 was spent in satisfying them. In April a force of 120,000 men was raised from the class of that year and another 100,000 from the recently annexed departments were taken from previous classes that had not been called up. In December 120,000 men were provided by the 1812 class, while the National Guard, composed of married men and of men not liable for active service, was called upon to supply a first contingent of 100,000 soldiers. The Emperor, it is true, gave an understanding that these men should not be sent out of France; nevertheless they were gradually moved to the garrisons on the Elbe, to Hamburg, Lübeck and to the furthest parts of the Empire. As soon as he arrived in Moscow and observed what wide gaps had been made in his army by the mere march there, he asked for 140,000 conscripts from the 1813 class.

Even these figures, however, do not represent the whole recruiting effort. They do not include the volunteers, the seventeen-year-old schoolboys who automatically became sergeant-majors, the soldiers' sons who became drummer-boys, the prisoners-of-war from the conquered countries, who had become French citizens, the émigrés who joined up in order to get their property back, the Chouans anxious to redeem their past by offering their services to Napoleon, or recaptured deserters, escaped or pardoned criminals who sought refuge from the law in the ranks of the army. The nation, stunned by such heavy sacrifices, which it felt to be useless, nevertheless put up with them because the Emperor's authority was great enough to coerce and to dazzle it. Yet every day confidence gave way to doubt, willingness to lethargy, resignation to simmering revolt.

If this was so in France, what could be said of the allies or satellites from whom the Emperor demanded ever-increasing contingents? Even when he was First Consul he used to raise regiments of Piedmontese, Ligurians, Dalmatians, Albanians, Swiss, Hessians and Dutch; he recruited a Polish legion and formed pioneer battalions with enemy deserters—real or supposed—and with negroes from San Domingo. But after Austerlitz, after Tilsit especially, foreign countries had to provide whole armies. Italy, of which Napoleon was king, was saddled with conscription, and half-yearly levies were imposed on Naples. Junot raised recruits in Portugal; Spain provided 15,000 men; the German princes of the Confederation of the Rhine were taxed at the rate of 120,000 men. Holland, despite the lamentations of Louis Bonaparte, had to produce first 25,000 and then 36,000 men. The Swiss cantons, of which the Emperor was the "Protector", had to find 16,000 soldiers. Poland raised large numbers of troops: 12 regiments of infantry, 9 of artillery and 3 of sappers, without counting the lancers of the Guard, the Galician bands, partisans and territorial units. For the Russian campaign alone the Grand Duchy raised 50,000 conscripts. In Vilna, Bassano endeavoured to organize Lithuanian units; while Prussia, still seething with hatred, and Austria, embittered though she was, were each forced to provide Napoleon with 30,000 men.

At the very beginning of the retreat from Russia Napoleon foresaw the disaster. For however wild his political dreams had become, in military matters he never lost touch with reality. On the day he left Moscow he began to concern himself with the question of finding replacements for the troops that he would lose during the retreat. The 10,000 men forming the first contingent of the National Guard, now stationed on the Elbe and the Oder, were embodied in the regular army "at their own request". He sent instructions to Paris for the immediate call-up of 100,000 conscripts from the earlier classes and, in addition, in order to replace his lost cavalry, for the provision of three mounted horsemen from each canton, making a total of 12,000 in all. "I have been offered these men," he declared. After Beresina he rushed back to Paris, leaving the army in charge of Murat. Public opinion was now up in arms against conscription, and the harassed civil service was at its wits' end to overcome resistance. As thousands of gendarmes, customs officers and foresters had been sent to the front to form the cadres for new units, they were no longer available for tracking down deserters. These rebels against conscription, becoming more numerous every day, formed bands which in some districts controlled parts of the countryside with the complicity of the local population.

By a decree of the Senate, dated January 11, 1813, the 1814 class was called to the colours: 150,000 young men of 18. A further decree imposed upon communes, towns, departments and state corporations a further levy of 15,000 fully-equipped men. On April 3 a new decree took 80,000 recruits from the classes already called and, in addition, raised 12,000 mounted "guards of honour" recruited from middle-class families irrespective of whether they had already paid for substitutes. This last measure, which hit the important people, caused more consternation than all the others together. In August, after the breakdown of the Pleisswitz armistice, a further batch of 120,000 men was called for from the earlier classes.

After Leipzig, in November 1813, Napoleon was back in Paris again, squeezing from an exhausted France the means for her defence. The August figure was increased by 30,000. Then he was granted another 300,000 to be taken from every class between 1803 and 1814, and, in the following month, 150,000 youths were called up from the 1815 class. The National Guard was mobilized and given its marching orders. In the east the Emperor declared a state of siege. He recalled veterans who had been demobilized years previously, including men who had been discharged as unfit, "provided they can stand up to cannon-fire and fire a musket". The figures stretched in never-ending lines, but not the soldiers. France in 1814 was gripped with a dreadful apathy. Despite the hateful invasion, her will-power, stretched for too long, suddenly broke. Bled white and crushed by a task of war-making to which she could see no end, she resigned herself to her fate, beaten already in her heart, hoping for a speedy end to her misery. Having taken three million men from the country, the Emperor was reduced at the decisive moment to a handful of soldiers.

In the war of masses which he had imposed upon himself, the quality of the troops had entered into an irreversible decline long before numbers began to fail. The flood of under-aged and unselected conscripts and foreigners with which the ever-widening gaps were filled were no substitute for the steady, toughened veterans who had neither the desire nor the time to train the raw material. The old regiments had been swallowed up by the Peninsular War, and the Emperor had fought his 1809 campaign with new formations. In the French army at Wagram one soldier in three was a foreigner, either a German or an Italian, the rest being recruits with less than eight months' service. Out of 600,000 men who crossed the Niemen, only half were French and, apart from the Guards, there was not one veteran in ten in any regiment. In 1813, at Lutzen, Bautzen, and Leipzig, the proportion was still smaller, despite the old soldiers recalled from Spain. With the exception of the Poles, all France's allies had abandoned her one by one.

As the physical quality of the troops deteriorated their morale was progressively weakened. For a long time the Emperor had succeeded in making them believe that the effort he was asking of them would be the last and that immediately afterwards they were going to be able to enjoy the fruits of victory. He had said it already at Marengo. "One last spurt," he declared to Oudinot's grenadiers at Hollabrünn, "and we have done it!" After Austerlitz he said: "Now you can go home!" At Tilsit he announced: "We've done with war," whereupon, we are told, "everyone went mad". When he led an army into Spain he held up before them the dazzling mirage of peace: "Your efforts will be rewarded by lasting peace and enduring prosperity," he proclaimed; and on the morning of the battle of the Moskowa; "Victory will give us abundance, good winter quarters and a speedy return to our own country." But as he was soon to realize, hope deferred maketh the heart sick. In the soldiers' mind the enthusiasm of yesterday gave way more and more to hopeless resignation. Sometimes it was kindled to bursts of anger. Even on the morrow of Eylau, when the Emperor passed in front of Saint-Hilaire's troops, who were incensed by the slaughter, he heard "ugly shouts". At the crossing of the Guadarrama, he passed by the division of General Lapisse, "whose men were howling on the ice-covered ground, swept by a biting wind, and daring one another to put a bullet through him". At Wiazma, after a retreat of two weeks over the Russian plain, as he watched the army pass, "from time to time the silence was broken by insults shouted at him". When, at Smorgon, he was leaving the army, according to an account of Ségur: "One can hardly imagine the dreadful insults hurled at the Emperor by the soldiers." "In 1813," wrote Coignet, "you didn't hear any singing in the ranks; only blaspheming and curses at the least bit of trouble. In December, near the bridge at Mainz, Napoleon watched the disorderly passage of the defeated troops from Leipzig. Seeing General Drouot, calm and loyal as ever, Napoleon went up to him and, tapping him on the chest, said: "I need a hundred men like that!" To which Drouot, with a glance at the disorderly throng, replied: "No, Sire, you need a hundred thousand."

Yet, despite their outbursts of irritability provoked by their sorry plight, the troops did their best; despite hardship and disillusion the great mass kept their sense of duty, and even their devotion to the Emperor, to the end. But willingness is not enough in war if it is unaccompanied by material strength, a factor which was constantly diminishing in the army of the Empire. How were the masses of conscripts which flowed into the depots to be trained, seeing that they had to be sent into the firing-line almost as soon as they were provided with uniform and weapons? From 1809 onwards this lack of training was painfully evident in the inelasticity of the troops and their lack of staying power in battle. On the evening of the battle of Eckmühl, when the Archduke Charles could have been driven back on to the Danube and destroyed, Napoleon, acting on the reports of his Marshals, had to give up the pursuit on account of the state of exhaustion in which the young soldiers were found. This lack of experienced troops was the chief cause of the heavy losses sustained at Essling: "Our formations remain deep, owing to the difficulty of deploying or concentrating untrained troops." Even before the Russian campaign Caulaincourt noted that "the front rank of the army cannot conceal the weakness of the other two". In 1813 the conscripts engaged at Lutzen had been on the march ever since they had left their homes. It is true that the Emperor had given orders that "no soldier shall leave until he has been under arms for a month and done some musketry drill." At the same time he expected to see young men who had been called up in France at the end of February assembled in Saxony in April! In any case, from now onwards he had to dispense with cavalry, with the result that his victories could never be clinched.

It was in the hope of repairing these grave deficiencies that he agreed to sign the Pleisswitz armistice. The Emperor used this breathing-space for training, and a great musketry competition was organized for the whole army. However, operations were resumed before any satisfactory results had been achieved. This was evident at the Katzbach, where Macdonald's regiments, which were scarcely organized at all, with "two thirds of the muskets out of order", were seized with wild panic. After Leipzig many units dispersed, and the Emperor complained of 70,000 deserters, who, in reality, were merely stragglers. The campaign in France was fought by a handful of veterans, remnants of the Spanish War and the Old Guard. The unfortunate conscripts who accompanied them can hardly be said to have reinforced him. At Champaubert the Marie-Louise Company of the 113th were leading. Marmont rode along the line and asked the men why they were not firing. "We can't shoot," was the reply. Another man said: "I'd have a go at firing if I had somebody to load for me." At Craonne the 2nd Division of the Young Guard found itself facing the Russians. General Boyer de Rébeval could only deploy his men in mass formation, for they had never learned any other kind of manœuvre. Meanwhile, in one battery "Drouot was showing a gunner, gently and calmly, how to train a gun."

Napoleon endeavoured to compensate for the progressive deterioration in the quality of his troops by increasing their armaments. "The poorer the troops the more artillery they need," he said. Thus, in 1806 he estimated that he needed

3,000 serviceable cannon; in 1809 he wanted double that number. Every campaign saw an increase in the general artillery reserve. At Austerlitz the French fired 50,000 rounds; at Wagram they fired 96,000; at the Moscawa, over 100,000; at Dresden the artillery of the Guard alone hurled 48,000 projectiles. The great artillerymen of the Empire, Sénarmont, Lariboisière, Drouot, excelled in these mass actions and were able, at first, to make up for lack of skilled troops by superior fire-power. But material wore out and replacements became progressively poorer in quality. The armaments industry suffered from lack of men, who, in any case, were badly paid. Botched work became more and more frequent. Twelve hundred cannon had been left behind in Russia and almost as many at Kulm, on the Katzbach and at Leipzig, without counting those that were abandoned by the roadside in Germany, Spain and Italy, and even in France. For the wood of which the gun-carriages and wheels were made, instead of being seasoned, as formerly, for ten, twenty or thirty years, now came from newly cut timber; as a result it warped, split and bent. As for the artillery from the fortified towns of France, multiplied by the Monarchy and by Carnot, Napoleon had taken it to equip the forts of the Elba, the Oder, the Vistula and the Quadrilateral. The infantry's armament also was deteriorating. It would have needed years to replace all the muskets lost in 1812 and 1813. Reserve stocks were locked up in Danzig, Stettin, Hamburg, Magdeburg or Dresden, with the result that during the campaign in France, according to Marmont, "the conscripts were given muskets with barrels that burst, touch-holes that were badly pierced or not pierced at all, and badly fitted triggers which produced constant misfires". The National Guard had sporting guns, and even pikes for the rear rank. At La Fère-Champenoise, recruits of Pacthod's division were mown down holding sticks in their hands.

If the Emperor had been able to count on lieutenants imbued, like himself, with the spirit of 1793, whose military worth gathered strength with adversity, fortune might have smiled on him again. But the zeal and loyalty of the leaders had not stood the test. They remained the valiant warriors they were, ready to take their lives in their hands and jealous, despite everything, of their military reputation; but they had lost their former fire just when it was most needed to warm the hearts of their weary troops. They now indulged in an ostentatious luxury which contrasted cruelly with the increasing wretchedness of the soldiers, and provoked them to acts of indiscipline. At the crossing of the Niemen the troops were furious at the sight of "the personal baggage of the king of Naples, drawn by a hundred horses, the baggage wagons and barouches of the marshals, the landaus and coupés of the generals, the two-in-hands or three-in-hands of the colonels, the cabriolets of the staff officers". Whenever certain great commanders found themselves on their own in occupied territory, they exhibited a disgraceful cupidity for which the Emperor reproved them, without putting an end to their conduct. And so their loyalty gradually crumbled away. No longer eager for action, they undertook it with minds troubled with personal preoccupations, reservations and suspicions. But as they were still afraid of their master and still anxious to get what they could from him, they were ready to deceive him in order to conceal their failings, surrounding Napoleon with exaggerations and boasts which invalidated his decisions. "The military reports", wrote Berthezène, "are suspect. Facts are tampered with for the sake of self-interest and vanity". The *Bulletin* itself had set the bad example and, ever since Eylau, had carefully concealed the truth.

Not that acts of daring and devotion were lacking. Lannes met his death at Essling, Bessières at Weissenfels, Duroc at Reichenbach. In Catalonia Suchet waged a magnificent campaign unaided. During the march on Moscow, Murat was still the dashing swordsman, always to be found among the leading scouts, amazing the enemy and his own cavalry as well by his dazzling outfits, indifferent to bullets and replying with a theatrical gesture to the distant salutes of the

Cossacks, "who took him for a magician and presented arms to him". During the retreat Ney performed miracles of heroism in the rearguard and continued to fight heroically until Waterloo. Elbé spent hours with the pontooners in the icy waters of the Beresina, an action which brought about his death a few days later; Oudinot, seriously wounded at Polotsk and suffering agonies in the saddle, made haste to join up with the army as soon as news of the retreat reached him; Gouvion-Saint-Cyr displayed the greatest resolution at Dresden, Davout defended Hamburg until peace was signed, Rapp won glory at Danzig, while, at Montereau, the veteran Lefebvre took part in the charge with such energy that "he foamed at the mouth"; Marmont worked untiringly as battalion commander during the whole campaign in France. Nevertheless, Napoleon complained that in Russia, "when there were more than nine degrees of frost he could not find a general at his post". Bernadotte betrayed him in 1813. In 1814 the king of Naples turned against his leader. At Leipzig, when a staff officer brought orders from the Emperor, Augereau shouted at him: "Does that b——y —— think that I am going to get myself killed or captured? Tell him from me that I'm not!" At Essounes Marmont led his troops over to the enemy lines. At Fontainebleau Ney, in an endeavour to force his master to abdicate, behaved "in an abominably violent manner", while Lefebvre, on leaving the Emperor's room, explained to the people he met: "I put the screw on pretty tight. Does he think that when we have got lands and titles and endowments we are going to get killed to please him? It's his own fault. He picked us out of the gutter too soon."

The decadence of his armies did not make the Emperor lose courage. He remained as clear-sighted, as confident and resolute at Wagram as at Marengo, at Lutzen as at Austerlitz, and in 1814 he was once more the general of the Italian campaign, sure of himself and indefatigable as ever. His will remained as unshakable in the depths of misfortune as at the height of success. But by striking too hard and too long he had broken the sword of France, for men's souls, like material things, suffer from wear and tear. Still undismayed, and still resolved to tempt providence once more, he suddenly found himself without soldiers or weapons, and saw, towering above him and ready to break, the swollen wave of ill will, of cowardice and treachery which was to engulf his genius.

His fall was as prodigious as his glory. The mind boggles at the thought of either. In the presence of such a stupendous career the judgment hesitates between blame and admiration. Napoleon left France crushed, invaded, drained of blood and courage, smaller than when he had taken control of her destinies, condemned to ill-drawn frontiers, the evils of which still persist, and exposed to the distrust of Europe which has weighed upon her to this day. But it is impossible to dismiss as of no account the matchless lustre which he imparted to our armies, the sure knowledge vouchsafed once and for all to his nation of her incomparable warlike qualities, the mighty reputation won for his country, the echoes of which still resound among mankind. No man had stirred human passions more profoundly, evoked fiercer hatreds or called forth more vehement denunciations. Yet few names have aroused such enthusiastic devotion that the very sound of it could stir men's souls. Napoleon exhausted the good-will of Frenchmen, abused their sacrifices and covered Europe with graves and ashes and tears; yet those who suffered most by him, even the soldiers, were his most faithful followers. Even today, despite the passing of time, shifts of opinion and new causes of mourning, crowds from every corner of the earth pay homage to his memory and feel the thrill of greatness as they stand beside his tomb.

Outraged reason exacted her inexorable vengeance; yet never did human genius and warlike virtue shine with such imperishable lustre.

FROM DISASTER TO DISASTER

THE EVENTS OF 1815 HAD LEFT FRANCE WITHOUT AN ARMY. SHE WAS FACED with the task of creating a new one at the same time as she rebuilt her other institutions. So violent had been the revolutionary upheaval, with such a profound effect on the soul of the nation, leaving so much bitterness between different sections of the community, that the reconstruction of society was achieved in an atmosphere of doubt and suspicion. Painful compromises had to be sought between the betrayals of the past and the principles of the present.

Conscription, having provided immense numbers of men who had been swallowed up by the wars of the Empire, had become, by its abuse, a hateful burden. All Napoleon's authority had been needed to maintain it. With the return of the Bourbons public opinion greeted with enthusiasm Article 12 of the Constitutional Charter, by which conscription was abolished, while the parties on the Right looked forward to a return to the army of the *ancien régime*. Recruiting was to be voluntary and the army's strength was to reside in its "quality". In fact, as Courtaval declared before the Representative Chamber to the great satisfaction of the reactionaries: "The family of European kings is reunited once more . . . Monarchical France has nothing to fear from Europe."

The liberal and left-wing parties, on the other hand, heirs of the Revolution, in their desire to undo the work of the Treaties of Vienna, continued to call for "quantity". "Would France," said Roger Collard, "fall a prey to nations that might wish to fall upon her? No. She would call upon all her sons. It is a right which has no need to be written and of which the Charter has been powerless to deprive her. Thanks to a uniform and simultaneous system of recruitment she will draw from her population those vast reserves of patriotic and nationally minded citizens who have endowed her with such glorious armies in the past."

The Gouvion-Saint-Cyr Act of 1818 struck the balance between these opposite tendencies. It did in fact proclaim that, to start with, recruiting would be on a voluntary basis, but conscription was nevertheless retained. However, the harshness of the life-blood tax was mitigated in favour of the privileged class of the day. The middle classes, whose political supremacy was assured by the electoral system, escaped from military service either by virtue of exemptions or by ransom. In point of fact the whole burden of military service fell on to the poorest classes. The load was lightened, however, by the fact that only a small part of the annual contingent was actually called up, the names being drawn by lot. And so for over half a century French society cheerfully put up with a system that let off many humble folk and left out altogether the people of influence and wealth.

But those who were affected bore a grievous burden; they were liable to six, seven or eight years' service, followed by the same length of time in the reserve after their demobilization. In his regiment a soldier was cut off from his family, among lads from every part of France, and changed from one garrison to another every eighteen months. Little was done for his comfort; he had to share a bed with a comrade and eat from a common bowl. He was subject to all the complicated rules and regulations of military duties and parades, sent to remove the barricades raised during disturbances in Paris and Lyons, despatched to fight in Spain, Morea, Algeria, Belgium, the Crimea, Italy, Syria, Mexico and China, and finally entrusted with the duty of guarding the frontier. Between 1820 and 1869 300,000 Frenchmen were killed in war. Only too often lack of imagination and negligence in high places added to the hardness of the soldier's lot. It needed ten years of Algerian heat and fevers and 2000 cases of suicide before authority abolished the heavy shako, the black horsehair collar and the straps crossed over the chest. Fifty thousand men perished in the Crimea before proper arrangements were made for feeding and sheltering the troops, while the neglect of the wounded in Italy is notorious. In return for these hardships the soldier received a miserable pittance of one *sou* a day. It was years before he could hope for the most modest promotion, while decorations rarely came his way. Until the Second Empire not a single private soldier received a distinction. The Military Medal was instituted in 1852 and the custom of distributing commemorative medals began only after the Crimea. A disabled soldier could become a pensioner at the Invalides, but a fit man was sent home without pension or gratuity once his term of service was up. He returned to his village to find his job gone and his girl married. In many cases he signed on again in return for a small cash payment, in the hope of becoming one day a policeman or clerk, a museum attendant or park-keeper.

At this period seventy-five per cent of the population of France lived in the country. The soldier was usually, therefore, a peasant, especially as the middle classes were exempt from military service, while the workmen from the towns were often medically unfit. These country lads brought with them a characteristic toughness and docility, combined with the vague thirst for adventure natural to their age and race. They accepted their bad luck stoically, and even cheerfully. The newly conscripted man would proudly display his registration number in his hat, deck himself out with ribbons and sing lustily. Once he was in the army, his service was so long and so unpredictable that he did not bother to count the days. In public he pulled himself together, for by the curiosity of the men, the glances of the women, and the admiration of the children he felt that he was an exceptional person. On his rare visits home, during his leaves or his six months' furlough, he took pride in the smartness of his uniform and the freedom of his expressions. In the field his gift for adaptation to circumstances was amazing. He accepted with equally good grace the forced marches of the African column, the war of attrition before Sebastopol, the great battles in Italy and the unfamiliarity of distant voyages. He even managed to show a certain amount of good humour in it all, celebrating in scores of ditties his pride in being a "Glazier" (*Vitriers*: the "chasseurs de Vincennes" were so called on account of their high knapsacks like a glazier's pack), a "Jackal", a "Porpoise" (*Marsouins*: Colonial infantry) or even a "Pebble-pusher", staging amateur theatricals in the sand of North Africa or the mud of Balaclava, marching to battle through Turin, Genoa, or Alexandria with a rose stuck in the muzzle of his gun, and blowing kisses to the balconies. In every climate, in all conditions, he greeted fate with the same slightly forced exuberance, the same philosophy touched with irony, that have found expression in the pungent and melancholy words he has fitted to his bugle-calls.

There was no more equality in the choice of officers than in the conscription of soldiers. Theoretically the epaulettes continued to be available to all. There were, too, a fair number of old soldiers who, thanks to the slaughter of the Napoleonic Wars, had been made officers, provided they could read and write their own name. But these old stalwarts died off in time, and were replaced by young men from the military colleges. By force of circumstances promotion, which during the great wars had been a question of courage and fighting ability, was now largely a matter of education. In practice most of the officers, especially in the higher ranks, were provided by middle-class families or by the old or the new aristocracy.

From their superiors and brother officers who had survived from the Empire these officers received strong military traditions, a taste for grandeur and confidence in the might of French arms. The Soult Act of 1832, by which their status was defined, removed them from the sphere of politics by confirming their commission and regularizing their position within the state. The party strife which they witnessed, the civil disturbances which they quarrelled, and all the other signs of disruption in the world around them had the effect of making them more devoted than ever to order, discipline and military stability. Their pay was poor, it is true, but the subaltern, who was nearly always a bachelor, had no commitments. He lived cheaply in the mess or hostel with the simplest appointments. This kind of life, which fostered comradeship and *esprit de corps* to a high degree, made the officer ready at any moment to leave for active service without anxieties or worries; but, on the other hand, it was prejudicial to serious study and to any other contacts with civilian society except those provided by balls and hunting. It came to be considered as something rather reprehensible for a military man to indulge in discussion, to show originality, or even initiative.

By their meticulous and absolute nature regulations were in keeping with the ideas of the time. An officer had only to consult them in any given situation to be told what course to pursue. He was thus spared the effort of making up his own mind. They conferred upon commanders the doubtful advantage of being able to act by the book rather than in the light of events. A few veterans of the Empire, having formed different habits, were at first loth to accept the tyrannous rule of regulations. But their resistance was of no avail. In 1833 at Perpignan, at the time of the Carlist wars, General de Castellane was inspecting the regiment of Colonel Combes. Knowing that they were due any day to march into Catalonia, Combes had taken it upon himself to relieve his men of a few of their impedimenta. Castellane stopped in front of the band. "Why are the sappers not wearing their aprons?" he asked. "Where is the big drum? Where are the Chinese bells and the serpents?" "As we do not need them for war," replied the colonel, "I had them left at the depot." "It is laid down in regulations that you must have them," was the reply, "you will send for them at once!"

Limited in their outlook and passive in their discipline, officers became less and less aware of general ideas, of the interdependence of things, and, in consequence, blind to the more complex aspects of action. Those who rose to the highest positions had not formed the necessary habit of applying their minds to a wide field of observation.

This weakness did not become evident at first. Men who, like Gouvion-Saint-Cyr, Marmont, Soult, Gérard and Mortier, had held high positions under the Empire, continued for decades to fill responsible military posts. Their immediate successors had fought long enough in the great wars as high-ranking officers to have preserved their instinct for leadership, while the Princes, who had played an effective part in the army of the Restoration and the July Monarchy, used their influence to favour the promotion of the best men. This was specially true in the case of the Dukes of Angoulême, Orléans and Aumale. Bugeaud again, by bringing his brilliant brain to bear on the lessons of his youth, acquired that sense of reality, that love of initiative, that tendency to rely on common sense and personal judgment rather than on theory and habit, which enabled him to adapt himself to the novel circumstances of the African war. Later, Saint-Arnaud proved himself capable of daring in large-scale enterprises. Pélissier showed inflexible and reasoned determination. But these exceptional personalities became fewer and fewer among the High Command. Baraguay-d'Hilliers, Canrobert, Bosquet, MacMahon, Bazaine and Bourbaki, brought to the forefront by the Algerian campaign, were brilliant as majors or colonels in handling small bodies of men. Having reached the High Command they still showed authority and strength, on condition that their task was strictly limited. A few generals, like Leboeuf and Frossard, who had served in the so-called "technical" sections of the army, became specialists and lost the wider view in an excess of technicalities. Still others, like Castelnau and Trochu, though gifted with exceptional intelligence, had applied it too long to administrative duties and had lost their sense of action.

Leaders who have never attained that high standard in the philosophy of their art which alone can give breadth of vision can never produce appreciations of wide application. They are destined to play subsidiary parts in the elaboration of any plan of campaign. The plans of 1854 and of 1859 were inspired respectively by the Englishman, Burgoyne, and the Swiss, Jomini. When left to their own devices our generals endeavoured to prepare themselves against eventualities, but were incapable of mastering events. In the Crimea, Canrobert showed a docile resignation. At Melegnano, Baraguay-d'Hilliers displayed a blind energy. In Mexico, Bazaine resorted to intrigue and dissimulation in order to hide his inefficiency.

So long as the army was fighting in Africa in relatively small groups against an indifferently armed enemy, the command could rely on its long familiarity with local conditions. But when whole armies were engaged in operations in Europe, the methods used in Africa were misleading. The army had a trained and conscientious General Staff. In this respect Martimprey, for example, showed exceptional abilities in the Crimea and in Italy. But the best general staff is powerless unless the commander has a clear plan. Thus the 1859 campaign was marked by every kind of blunder and negligence in its preparation. The concentration of troops on the Doria and at Genoa was attended by confusion. During the whole campaign our troops were fed less by the foresight of the Commander-in-Chief than by the kindness of the inhabitants of Lombardy. In 1867 Napoleon III assembled all the highest and most reputable officers in the army at the Camp of Châlons. It was resolved that they would work out a plan of campaign together. But in order to do so they would have had to have a framework of the general plan, they would have had to make an appreciation of the situation and finally to give the necessary orders. But as nobody there was capable of evolving any such plan, the Emperor adopted the course of asking General Trochu to read aloud some passages from the work of Thiers on *The History of the Consulate and the Empire*.

The commanders were untiring in the execution of their duties. It is true that, for want of a sound method, their zeal often prevented them from distinguishing between essentials and non-essentials, and impelled them to make unnecessary personal interventions and to become embroiled in details to the detriment of the whole. But, whatever their rank, they showed a complete disregard for their personal safety. When three assault columns were to enter Constantine, their three colonels, Lamoricière, Combes, and Corbin, sword in hand, were literally the first to enter the breach. At Sebastopol seventeen generals were killed. MacMahon scaled Malakoff behind the first wave of his division. Knowing that the fort was mined, he remained near his divisional flag, and the sight of him kept the terrified soldiers at their posts. At Magenta, General Regnault de Saint-Jean d'Angély, General Cler and General Mellinet constantly walked about among the sharpshooters of the Guard who were bearing the whole brunt of the battle. Thanks to this attitude on the part of the leaders, their troops knew them and trusted them. But sometimes the hardships suffered by the sorely-tried soldiers led to demonstrations. After the Dobruja expedition, while Saint-Arnaud was reviewing three divisions which had been decimated by cholera, there were shouts of: "What were we sent here for? To die of cholera? Send us back to Africa or against the Russians!" Pélissier was booed by the columns returning from the fruitless attack on Sebastopol on June 18. On the day before the battle of Magenta the division commanded by General Espinasse loudly demanded food and rest. Lapses of this kind, however, were of no great significance. They were offset, on the other hand, by a certain cordial familiarity. Marshal Bugeaud was not in the least offended by jokes about his famous cap. The Turcos were wont to celebrate their leader in a ditty which ran something like this:

*Why are Turcos so snappy
And their girl-friends so happy?
It's thanks to that chappie
Called Charlie Bourbaki.*

At Magenta Marshal Canrobert was among the Grenadiers of the Guard when they began to cheer him as they fired. The Marshal, "doffing his képi with a theatrical gesture, and throwing back his big head with its long wavy hair and turned-up moustache", replied to the cheers with: "Greetings, gentlemen of the Guard!" whereat the enthusiasm of the grenadiers knew no bounds.

These hard-bitten soldiers who had learned to expect nothing for their services, these officers who revelled in action but recoiled from hard work, made a tough but uninspired army, first-rate for a limited task in which the men's endurance and the inventiveness of the officers found their full scope and produced the happiest results. But an army of that calibre could not stand the test of a large-scale war.

II

As the instrument of a policy of realism and moderation the army would have been entirely adequate. This was, in fact, the purpose for which it had been formed by the government of the Restoration. By "forging anew the links with the past" the monarchy intended to resume its traditional foreign policy: to preserve the European balance of power, to hinder the formation of great powers on the French frontiers—above all, to keep Germany divided; to form alliances based on self-interest, to attract the adhesion of the small powers, to extend gradually towards the Rhine, consolidating every step before embarking on new ventures, to maintain supremacy in the Mediterranean and to prevent any naval hegemony in the Atlantic. For the purpose of the small-scale interventions, preventive operations and long-distance expeditions necessitated by a policy of this nature, the army constituted by the Acts of Gouvion-Saint-Cyr and Soult was adequate and necessary. It gained the respect without arousing the alarm of Europe, was ready to perform its function of waging war without enquiring into motives, and to fight at any time or anywhere, and proved highly satisfactory in Spain, Morea and Algeria.

But from 1830 onwards an ever-increasing current of opinion favoured a more enterprising policy abroad. Not for nothing had France drunk her fill of glory in the days of the Revolution and the Empire. The renewal of the caution of the *ancien régime* seemed to many patriots an anachronism. The treaties of 1815 seemed to them to imply the acceptance of a humiliation which must at all costs be obliterated. France, they said, had "settled in the mud". Under the impulsion of these memories, ambitions and grievances, men's minds were stirred with the desire for a more grandiose policy. The ideas of the "Action" party were becoming more and more accepted; France should take as her guiding principle not the national interest, but an abstraction, such as liberty, justice, nationality; she should listen more readily to sentiment than to reason; she should embark upon a course of action, provided it seemed good and right, and damn the consequences. "France is bored," said Lamartine; while Armand Carrel denounced what he called "the cowardly system that proclaims the political egoism of France". The July Monarchy was able to resist the tendency; the desire for enterprise was humoured by the expeditions of Antwerp and Ancona and by the conquest of Algeria.

But Napoleon III made a clean break with traditional policy. The siege of Sebastopol and the expulsion of the Austrians from Lombardy were, it is true, limited objectives, in the attainment of which the army acquitted itself honourably. But by promoting the formation of two great new powers on the frontiers,

B

contributing to the weakening of Russia and Austria, and allowing the European equilibrium to be upset, the Emperor was preparing all the conditions for a conflict in which France would have to defend her soil and her future by her own resources. To wage a national war of this nature France would have needed quite another kind of army.

The Emperor was conscious of the shifting of the balance. After Sadowa, seeing that war against Prussia, strengthened by the German states, was becoming inevitable, Napoleon III and several of his advisers gave their serious attention to the country's military potential. Already in 1866, profiting by the shock caused by the new Prussian needle-gun, the Emperor had given orders for the introduction of the chassepot, which had been invented eleven years earlier but turned down by the experts of the Artillery Committee as being "quite useless for service purposes". The rifled barrel had been adopted in exactly similar conditions, just as, in 1869, the machine-gun was put into production on the orders of the Emperor. But the improvement of weapons was not the only important question. The Emperor, who saw quite clearly that the whole organization of the army needed overhauling, wished to bring in compulsory short-term military service on the Prussian model in order to make the army numerically strong. Here again the reform came up against the two usual obstacles: public opinion, which opposed any increase in taxation, and the objections of the technicians to any change in the familiar order of things.

At first, yielding to opposition, the Emperor gave up the idea of a general system of conscription and supported the hand-to-mouth plans of Marshal Niel for the retention of long-term military service and the formation of a mobile National Guard, which was to be given a summary training and drafted into the regular army in the event of mobilization.

The plan was attacked both by the Prefects and by the *Conseils Généraux*. As soon as the bill was proposed it was mangled by the Council of State and when it came up for debate in the Legislative Assembly it became a party matter, openly attacked by the opposition on the Left, who denied the danger of war and called on the government to abolish the standing army, and secretly opposed by the Right, who feared its effect on the already growing unpopularity of the government. "For my own part," said Jules Simon, "I do not believe that war is imminent, for Prussia has no interest in making war on France." The German army, contended Emile Ollivier, is an essentially defensive army. "We are obliged to pass the bill", wrote an official deputy, "because the Emperor wants it, but we shall see to it that the law is inoperative." As a result the Mobile Guard, for which the minister had first of all demanded four months' training, and then seventy-five days, was finally subject to the following regulation: "The Guard cannot be mustered more than fifteen times a year. No muster may entail more than one day's absence from work. Young men who satisfy the authorities that they are proficient in the use of weapons are exempt."

Many of the soldiers showed no more understanding of the situation than the politicians. In the early days of his reign Napoleon III had drafted a bill for recruitment by districts and for the call-up of reservists in the nearest town to their home, a measure designed to simplify the operation of a mobilization order. The military committee to which the suggestions were submitted, however, rejected them. Its secretary, Colonel Trochu, concluded his report with these words: "An army of this kind would be a national army; that is something we do not require." Niel's plan met strong opposition from the army. The military commission appointed to examine it could not agree. "These proposals," said Marshal Randon, "will give us only recruits. It is soldiers we need!"

The plan for reorganizing the armed forces was therefore changed out of all recognition. The death of the minister who had formulated it, together with the general state of inertia, prevented the enforcement even of the small part that remained of it. The Mobile Guard was never mustered, except for a few days, in Paris. In 1870 France, armed for a local war, was plunged into a war of nations.

In contrast to their French contemporaries, the German authorities had made their army into a most efficient instrument. William, on his accession in 1861 to the throne of Prussia, after his regency, had given his whole mind to the task. While Bismarck, appointed Chancellor in 1862, was bringing about the political conditions of victory, Roon, War Minister from 1858, and Moltke, Chief of General Staff from 1861, were forging the military conditions. The campaigns of 1864 and 1866 had put the existing organization to a severe test. Every citizen served three years in the regular army (one year only if he belonged to one of the liberal professions) and then passed into the reserve and, later, the *Landwehr*. He was automatically called out at the first mobilization order. This system, imposed by William as Regent, in the teeth of bitter opposition from Parliament, was extended to the confederation of northern states and completed after Sadowa by military agreements with the southern states, and gave the Prussian commander a force of over a million men at the very beginning of hostilities.

It was an army of docile troops, led by officers taken almost exclusively from among the Prussian landed gentry, forming a homogeneous body both by reason of their social standing and of their devotion to the reigning dynasty, supported by the king, who wore their uniform; by the princes, who served in their ranks; and by the public authorities, who saw in them the bulwark of the state. This haughty and exclusive caste might have provided a fertile soil for routine and for an exaggerated admiration of the past had not a great soldier made of it a training school for talent. Conscious that the conduct of operation in modern warfare demands intellectual qualities of a high order, Moltke had given his whole mind and energy to the formation of a General Staff, recruited from the best officers leaving the Military Academy. Its quality was maintained by a constant process of selection, and its efficiency was ensured by exercises and missions of all kinds designed to fit it for the task of handling the complicated military machine.

Thus the French army, which a weak government had been unable to reform, found itself on the outbreak of war faced with a well-prepared enemy. The mobilization order of July 14, 1870 had resulted in the arrival of 250,000 men on the frontier on August 5; 60,000 were in their depots or else in Algeria or Rome. Nothing more could be expected for several months. Worse still, these forces were organized, armed and transported in chaotic conditions, for since no large units were in existence in peacetime, the task of forming them had to be undertaken from A to Z on the frontier; they had to be allotted staffs, cannon, ammunition, wagons and material of all kinds. During this time the enemy brought up for the first encounters 500,000 men already organized into army corps and divisions, manned his depots with a further 160,000 soldiers, and called up a well-disciplined *Landwehr* of 100,000 men.

The French had no superiority in armaments to offset their numerical inferiority. It is true that the chassepot was a better rifle than the dreyse; it had a higher rate of fire and its flat trajectory made its fire more deadly. But there were two German infantrymen to every one on the French side. The German artillery was far and away the better. Instead of the 900 cannon of the French, the Germans had 1,500. Every German gun was capable of firing 450 times, whereas the French guns could fire no more than 280. The German weapons were superior both in range and precision. The French, on the other hand, had machine-guns, bullet-firing weapons secretly manufactured at Meudon, on which the most extravagant hopes were placed. There had been no opportunity, however, of studying their use, and their chief value was to be chiefly moral, by virtue of the illusions which were entertained as to their mysterious power.

Yet, such as it was, the French had a keen and hardened army which constituted a powerful instrument. In the hands of resolute leaders it could have snatched success, if not victory, from many an opportunity. But whereas the German masses were directed by a clear, well-conceived plan, the French forces were bandied to and fro by contradictory orders.

Before the war the "Archduke Albert" plan for the offensive and the plan of General Frossard for the defensive had remained in the state of proposals. The Emperor and his advisers had come to no definite conclusions. To begin with, therefore, they contented themselves with stringing out the troops all along the frontier. On August 6 an isolated army corps was defeated at Froeschwiller, when it would have been easy to concentrate three. At Forbach the 2nd Corps was reduced to its three divisions, when an order, given in time, could have put seven into the line.

After this unfortunate beginning, followed by a week of vacillation, the High Command decided to concentrate all its forces in the field. Bazaine received orders from the Emperor to bring back the army from Metz to Verdun in order to join up with the troops from Alsace which were being re-formed by MacMahon at the Châlons Camp. At last it would seem that the fine French divisions were to be grouped and given the requisite flexibility for manœuvre. But for that Marshal Bazaine would have had to know how to move, encamp and supply a body of 180,000 men; how to reconnoitre, how to organize defence and liaisons. Of this he was incapable. Feeling his incapacity, but refusing to admit it—and herein lay his greatest fault—he saw fit to do nothing and to cling to an obstinate and unimaginative system of inaction.

Learning that Bazaine was immobilized, Marshal MacMahon prepared to fall back on Paris. There, his experienced troops would be joined by the new forces which were being raised in all parts of the country, and the national defence could then be organized. But the Regency government, terrified at the political consequences of a retreat of such dimensions, ordered him to march on Montmédy to the aid of Bazaine. Twice MacMahon broke off the movement, and twice he was ordered to continue; and so this ill-conceived plan, hindered at every turn, succeeded in placing round Sedan, in a situation fraught with mortal danger, a distracted Commander-in-Chief and a bewildered army. While the battle was actually in progress three commanders took charge of operations in turn, each adopting measures which cancelled out the earlier ones. The first commander, MacMahon, wanted to hold his ground; the second, Ducrot, decided to fall back on Mezières; the third, Wimpffen, launched an offensive in the direction of Carignan.

This infirmity of purpose gave rise to tragic mistakes in execution. The absence of adequate precautionary measures on August 4 at Wissembourg, the march of the army of Metz on August 15 along one road when three might have been used, the failure of the cavalry to intervene, on August 15 and 16, while the army was in retreat, the tangle into which the columns of the Châlons army got themselves during the march on Montmédy, the lack of any serious cover for the 5th Corps during its halt near Beaumont on August 30—all these blunders contained the germ of future disaster.

Not that the enemy's tactics were always irreproachable; on several occasions he was in such an awkward situation that a little local initiative on the part of the French commanders would have put him in serious danger. But there is always a way out if one's adversary remains passive. Having no specific orders, MacMahon at Froeschwiller and Frossard at Spicheren contented themselves with defending the positions they occupied. At the same time, Failly and Bazaine, who could have marched towards the sound of the cannon, failed to do so, or did so too late. On August 16 Canrobert, who had engaged his main forces to the west of Rezonville, and saw quite well that his right wing, by advancing on Trouville Wood, could easily outflank the 3rd Prussian Corps and bring about a decision, scrupulously refrained from taking the necessary action, because he had received no orders to that effect, and remained at his commander's post on the Roman Way, imperturbably smoking one cigar after another amidst a hail of cannon-fire. Ladmirault, who shortly afterwards debouched further to the right with 30,000 men who could have made victory certain had they been sent forward, contented himself with local gains, for fear of going counter to the intentions of the High Command.

The commanders, men experienced in many campaigns, were by no means devoid of talents. Placed as they were in a most unenviable situation, they frequently gave proof of resourcefulness. The positions both at Froeschwiller and Spicheren were well-chosen. General Bataille's counter-attacks round Stiring on August 6 were models of vigour and timeliness. No exception could be taken to the dispositions ordered by Ducrot to cover the retreat of the 1st Corps at Neiderbronn. On August 14, before Mey, Ladmirault conducted the engagement of his 4th Corps with great skill. On August 16 the entire action of Cissey's division—the approach march behind the fighting line, the debouchment and the engagement near the Cuve ravine—is deserving of the highest praise.

What is more, following a noble tradition, the French generals exposed themselves unhesitatingly to fire, as if they hoped to compensate by personal valour for their lack of method and means. At Froeschwiller MacMahon spent the whole day in the most exposed observation posts. On August 16 Bazaine moved about in the firing-line with great courage, massing a battalion here, placing a battery there. On August 18 Canrobert, who was defending Saint-Privat, remained with his sharpshooters during the whole battle, withdrawing only with the last échelon. At Sedan, Wimpffen, on foot and sword in hand, endeavoured up to the last moment to hack his way towards Balan, leading the groups of soldiers that he had been able to collect in three assaults. On the battlefields of Alsace, Lorraine, and the Ardennes, a Marshal of France and twenty generals were killed. The honour of the leaders was saved thereby. What they lacked was neither experience nor courage, but farsightedness, depth of judgment and breadth of outlook. Without these qualities the problems presented by a large-scale war are insoluble.

Yet, despite their weakness in effectives, despite their almost hopeless strategical and tactical dispositions, despite the demoralization engendered among the lower ranks by vacillation in the higher command, the troops on the battlefield showed themselves so tough and so resolute that defeat, though losing nothing of its bitterness, yet assumed a certain grandeur. Most of the officers, many n.c.o.s and a certain number of private soldiers had already fought, with the result that their regiments had acquired a certain degree of cohesion. The story of those tragic days is full of gallant actions, sprung from brilliant, warlike qualities. The counter-attacks launched by the 1st Tirailleurs at Wissembourg on August 4, and, two days later, to the east of Froeschwiller, the stubborn fight of the 3rd Zouave Regiment at the Niederwald and the counter-blow struck by the 8th Line Regiment against the Gifertwald at Spicheren, the capture of Mey Wood by Grenier's division at Borny on August 14, the vigorous action north of Vionville on August 16 by the artillery of the 2nd Corps, the defence of Roncourt and Saint-Privat by the divisions of Levassor-Sorval and Lafont de Villiers and by the 9th Line Regiment, the fight put up by the Marines at Bazeilles and at Balan, the cavalry charges at Morsbronn and Floing: feats of arms such as these have never been surpassed by any army at any time.

These gallant men strove by sheer courage to counter the blows of an evil fate. Knowing full well what they were doing, they rushed gladly to arms when they were called; on August 14, during the retreat to the Moselle, they turned about when they heard the cannon, scaled the plateaux of Borny and Saint-Julien at the run, so fired with enthusiasm that some of the soldiers wept with emotion; on August 16, east of Mars-la-Tour, feeling that the enemy, exhausted and outflanked, was near breaking-point, yet hampered themselves by inexplicable orders to do nothing, they raised a shout of "Forward!" along the whole line. They were steadfast and undaunted by every setback. They fought as bravely at Saint-Privat as at Spicheren; bottled up in Metz and seeing disaster approaching, they fought at Noisseville and at Ladonchamps as if hope still remained undimmed. Despite the absurd use that was made of them, outnumbered by two to one, crushed by the enemy's superior artillery, they handled their weapons so well that, during the first three great weeks of August they killed or wounded 58,000 of the enemy, losing 49,000 themselves. These loyal men paid by humiliation and wretchedness for the mistakes of others; returning from the prison-camps in which they had been herded by the enemy, they summoned up enough devotion and discipline to tear down the barricades of the Commune and save the state. The undeserved misfortunes of these gallant men remain as a grim yet salutary warning to all who hold the reins of government or military command.

III

When, on the morning of September 2, Bismarck asked Napoleon III if the sword which the Emperor was handing over to the King of Prussia was the sword of France, he had no doubt that the German victory would shortly be crowned by peace. From the purely material point of view, indeed, all resistance was impossible. Yet France was to raise new armies and carry on the struggle for another five months, saving thereby her honour if not her prestige.

The national defence, however, had to be organized under the most unfavourable conditions. Vainly did the Regency Government, on August 7, after the first setbacks, call upon Frenchmen "to recognize one party only, that of France"; political passions were unleashed, and the Imperial régime was unable to survive the news of Sedan.

The war had, therefore, to be carried on by a makeshift government. The efforts of the National Defence were hampered by the confusion caused by such a sudden and complete changeover. The men of the Republican opposition who had seized power did not possess the requisite authority for their task. They were distinguished neither by their political ideals, which were by no means shared by the majority of the country, nor by their talents, which they had so far had no opportunity of showing except on the platform. Nor can it be said that they were remarkable for their foresight, seeing that up to the last moment they had failed to recognize the Prussian danger and had opposed the reform of the army. What is more, in their anxiety to establish the new régime, they upset the existing administration in order to fill the vacant posts with their own place-seeking followers, thus multiplying a hundredfold the grievous disadvantages inherent in a revolution accomplished in the presence of the enemy.

Yet despite all their mistakes, due to ideology, prejudice, and lack of experience, the Government of National Defence did in fact undertake the direction of the war. It raised men, gathered material, found leaders and imposed its own plans. It is true that this was not accomplished without inefficiency and waste, for there can be no substitute for method and knowledge. But the Government did what it set out to do and, notwithstanding all the disappointments inseparable from improvisation, it is to these men that France is indebted for the moral benefit she gained from the prolongation of the struggle.

This national resurgence is identified with the person of Gambetta. When, on October 9, the young deputy arrived at Tours in order to assume the direction of the war in the provinces, he had had no experience which fitted him for this crushing task. However, he had faith in himself and strove to compensate for his lack of knowledge of practical affairs by his eloquence, his enthusiasm and his determination; an eloquence composed of metaphors rather than reasoning, yet pregnant with ideas; an ostentatious enthusiasm, rooted less in intellectual convictions than in a fiery temperament, yet communicating itself to others and sweeping away doubts in its flood; a reckless determination, but one which overcame the prevailing inertia and flabbiness. Gambetta, in short, though headstrong rather than enlightened, and active rather than diligent, yet succeeded in bringing to bear the weight of a powerful personality. He possessed gifts of leadership and knew how to make use of them at a time when France was foundering for want of direction.

After Sedan there were practically no more French troops in the field. Bazaine's army, hopelessly cut off near Metz, was entering upon its death agony. Twenty-five thousand men under Vinoy, having failed to join up with MacMahon, were retreating from Mézières towards the capital. In Paris a further 30,000 were assembled with great difficulty from the depots, with over 14,000 sailors, and the same number of gendarmes, customsmen and foresters. In Algeria the colony was guarded by a few battalions and cavalry squadrons. That represented the sum total of trained and organized men which could be set against the million victorious German soldiers advancing into French territory.

Although the army depots contained 145,000 men, this figure included 90,000 conscripts of the 1869 class who had been called to the colours only a month previously, 15,000 tradesmen and clerks, and 10,000 unfit men. The Mobile Guard, which was mustered at the beginning of August, consisted of 365,000 young men. The 1870 class, called up in October, provided 160,000 recruits. Thirty thousand men had signed on for the duration. In November there was a call-up of what was known as the "Mobilized" National Guard; single men or childless widowers of thirty-five. In the fortified towns, more especially in Paris, the National Guard performed a number of duties, and finally, certain auxiliary formations, partisans, Pontifical Zouaves and the Legions of Garibaldi made their contribution to resistance. In this way France, a country where, for fifty-five years, the mass of the nation had been exempt from military service, afforded striking evidence of her vitality by giving so many of her sons to meet the emergency. But until they could receive training they represented little more than a shapeless mass.

The Government of National Defence and, above all, its Provincial Delegation, employed every effort to organize this host. Between September 4, 1870 and February 2, 1871 over a million men, forming seventeen army corps and several independent divisions, were thrown in against the enemy. This result was all the more remarkable since all decisions and preparations had to be made at the centre, for the former military zones no longer existed, and the new prefects to whom fell the task of recruiting and organizing units proved to be incompetent. Moreover, the Delegation found considerable difficulty in preventing their forces from splitting up into irregular formations. Fortunately certain bodies, such as the "Francs-Tireurs of the Atlas", the "Marseilles Guerillas", the "Republican Chasseurs of the Loire", the "Bears of Nantes", and the "Mountain Irregulars" were exceptions to this rule.

If there had existed, at least, good cadres of officers to lead these scratch troops, the soldier's adaptability might, up to a certain point, have compensated for his lack of knowledge and training. But the greatest need was for officers. The ordinary rules for promotion had to be waived; commanders were appointed at random as the need arose, officers on the retired list were recalled, and commissions given to every n.c.o. who could be discovered in barracks, depots, and stores. An auxiliary cadre was formed in order to incorporate into the army naval officers and suitable men from civilian employment to serve in the administration, engineers and postal services. On the other hand, there appeared in the higher ranks people whose chief qualifications were their political friendships, and others who were mere adventurers unfitted in every way for their positions. In the Mobile Guard the officers, who at first had been appointed by the Minister of War, were chosen after September 4 by election. Fortunately the men showed sense enough in nearly every case to confirm the previous nominations, with the result that the cadres of these young battalions were, as a rule, reasonably good.

The Ordnance Department at Tours, under the direction of General Thoumas and Colonel de Reffye, performed miracles of hard work and ingenuity in arming these vast numbers of troops. In Paris the War Minister, Palikao, had by August amassed great stores of material, while the capital's productive capacity was able to provide the rest on the spot. Elsewhere, however, things were very different. In October the stores provided 120,000 chassepot rifles, while a further 200,000 were in existence in the depots. In addition, the factories turned out 20,000 a month. This total was insufficient to provide a rifle for every infantryman. The National Guards, the "Mobilized" men and certain mobile battalions had to be issued with *fusils à tabatières*—muskets converted into breech-loaders—which, although quite useful weapons and almost as good as the Dreyse rifle, were unpopular with the men, who were aware that better rifles existed. Above all, the government had to buy from abroad anything that foreign countries were willing to sell them. At the time of the armistice the French troops were armed with no fewer than eighty-nine different patterns of rifles.

As regards artillery the situation was little better. It is true that the arsenals provided over a thousand pieces of ordnance, but these did not represent batteries, since there were neither gun-carriages, ammunition wagons, gunners, horses nor harness. The National Defence did finally succeed in putting 2,200 field-guns into the line, with the necessary equipment and artillery parks, but the relation between the quantity of material and the use that could be made of it was remote.

It was no easy task to lead such heterogeneous troops into battle. Most of the new units were commanded by generals who, like Ducrot, Martin des Pallières, Clinchamp, Bourbaki or Cambriels, had either escaped or had been released from captivity on account of wounds or some other chance circumstance, or who, like d'Aurelles de Paladines or Vinoy, were taken from the reserves, or again, like Chanzy, Sonis, Faidherbe, Farre and Crouzat, had remained at first in Algeria, in the colonies, or in the interior of France. Nearly all of them did their best with the defective material at their disposal, but others lost courage in the bewildering and unfamiliar circumstances. Several naval officers, such as La Roncière Le Nourry, Jaurèguiberry, Jaurès and Gougeard, exercised great common sense and authority in acquitting themselves of their unforeseen task. And lastly, among the improvised generals, men like Charette or Garibaldi gave proof of talent; others, like Crémer or Clément-Thomas, were busy rather than efficient; whilst yet others, like Robin or Crévisier, were simply incapable.

Nevertheless, in those grim days, when those in command were faced not only with a victorious enemy but with all the adverse circumstances which dog the steps of every attempt at improvisation, there emerged leaders who wielded their broken sword with vigour. D'Aurelle made the Army of the Loire into a reliable fighting force. Thanks to him, at Coulmiers, "the genius of France was reborn". Although at Beaune-la-Rolande, Loigny and Orleans he was worsted by the veterans of Frederick-Charles, he did at least keep control of the engagement and organize the retreat in good order. Near Paris, Ducrot made the best of a hopeless situation. Although failing in their object of raising the siege, Champigny and Buzenval were both soundly prepared and well-conducted operations. In the north, Faidherbe, in the course of a vigorous campaign, struck the enemy hard at Pont-Noyelles and Bapaume, and succeeded after Saint-Quentin in saving his troops. As Gambetta said of him: "He thinks and he looks ahead, a rare enough quality in these days!" Cambriels, too, showed a real understanding of war in his operations in the Vosges and in the Franche-Comté.

But it was Chanzy who, more than any other man, succeeded in adapting his talents and his knowledge to the new circumstances. He brought his instinct of war into relation with his general knowledge of events. His soul remained steadfast, so that amidst the most trying circumstances and the worst disasters he retained "that calmness in adversity" which, according to Voltaire, "is Nature's supreme gift to a commander". At Coulmiers and Villepion he showed great skill in leading the young troops of his 16th Corps. As Commander-in-Chief of the 2nd Army of the Loire after the loss of Orleans, he hung on to the Josnes lines with his hard-pressed troops, reformed them while the battle was still in progress, and held the best German troops in check for four days. The retreat to the Loire which he subsequently had to undertake with a decimated army, over abominable country and in dreadful weather, was a masterpiece of coolness. The later retreat to Mons, carried out by exhausted troops, would have been transformed into a rout had it not been for the general's foresight and determination. No sooner had his army been restored before he made an attempt to harass the enemy by means of mobile columns. Under heavy attack in the lines at Le Mans, he repulsed the enemy again and again. Thrown back as far as Laval, he prepared to fight again. If it had been possible for one man to change the fate of France, that man would have been Chanzy.

In fact, France, with its wealth of resources, could in time have acquired the means of regaining the initiative. The war was lost, but another war might have been won if only there had been time. Time was needed to organize, arm and train the new masses of recruits and to select their leaders. Time was needed to set the administration of the army going again, to rouse the sympathies of Europe and to amass supplies. Time was needed to tide over that dreadful winter of 1870–71 without risking any decisive operations. But time was not available. The blockade of Paris had to be broken. Owing to the part played by the capital in the life of the nation, the memories of 1814, the theory of entrenched camps, due to Rogniat and popularized by the Belgian general Brialmont, and owing to the personality of Trochu, the Governor, a large army and a considerable amount of material had been concentrated in the city. Moreover, the government of September 4 was the result of an agitation in Paris, being composed of Paris deputies and including the Governor of the city. It tended, therefore, to identify the fate of the country with that of its capital. By allowing her government and the major part of her resources to be shut up within the great city, France defined the meaning and the limits of her resistance. For despite the spirit of sacrifice shown by the population, the supplies within the walls of the city were by no means inexhaustible. The date at which surrender was inevitable was fixed by the Governor, first for the middle of December, and then for mid-January. This inexorable time limit was to compromise everything by obliging the country to act with undue haste.

This was evidenced by the offensive launched in November by the Army of the Loire, and intended to coincide with a sortie by the Paris garrison. Vainly did d'Aurelle plead that his forces were scattered and his preparations incomplete. He had to act, and act quickly, since Paris demanded it. And although this first attempt at the offensive was rewarded by the victory of Coulmiers, it was an incomplete victory; the troops were unable to exploit their success, owing to their lack of experience in manœuvre.

A few days later, first at Beaune-la-Rolande and then at Loigny, the same reasons provoked the same haste. It became known that the Army of Paris was engaged in a big-scale sortie. On the pretext of saving time the Delegation gave orders direct to the various army corps. The right wing, sent forward without any co-ordination with the left wing, was held up in front of the German lines; whereupon the left wing tried, in vain, to go over to the offensive, while the right stayed where it was. Having been defeated section by section, the Army of the Loire was no longer able to hold its positions round Orleans.

But, despite his successes, the enemy too was exhausted. With constantly diminishing effectives and ever-waning enthusiasm, he waged a hard winter campaign in which every victory was costly without being decisive, in which communications remained precarious and skirmishes between the main battles gave him no rest. The Army of Paris, the two Armies of the Loire, the corps engaged in operations in the east, the formations in Normandy and Brittany, and, finally, the Army of the North might have struck hard blows if only they could have struck together. A general offensive demanded time for its preparation, but the government considered that delay was impossible. It consequently adopted a plan for cutting the enemy's communications in the east: an unorthodox operation, but one capable of being carried out without delay. While, therefore, the Army of the East set out amidst the general confusion to attempt a risky decision at the other end of the country, Chanzy at Le Mans, Ducrot at Buzenval, and Faidherbe at Bapaume and Saint-Quentin were wearing themselves out in unco-ordinated efforts.

It was evident that this fumbling strategy was entirely inadequate to make good use of the forces available. Gambetta demanded swift and heavy blows, struck continuously and at all points; Chanzy approved and Freycinet gave orders to this effect. But for his orders to be carried out the troops would have had to be of a very different calibre. Disorder set in as soon as they began to march; the roads were strewn with men crippled with their packs, their boots, their equipment, while isolated groups fought little wars of their own. To make things worse, the supply services functioned badly or not at all, and the soldiers were constantly engaged in plunder. To avoid the danger of dispersal, cantonments were rarely used; the troops bivouacked in the November mud and rain, in the cold and the snow of December and January. The state of health among the men was consequently deplorable. When there was fighting to be done, much time was consumed in forming the columns, approaching the enemy and opening fire. This factor weighed so heavily that when an encounter was to be expected, certain generals deployed their units long in advance, preferring the difficulties of marching across country to those involved in deploying in a hurry.

However, once the commanders had put their men in their places and sited the artillery, providing always that they commanded the main action in person, the troops showed considerable dash in the early stages of the battle. At Coulmiers, the storming of La Renardière by General Peytavin's division and the capture of the village itself by the 7th Battalion of Chasseurs, the 38th and the *Mobiles* of the Dordogne; the capture, some days later, of Villepion by General Jauréguiberry's division, the charge on Loigny by the Pontifical Zouaves, the *Mobiles* of the Côtes-du-Nord and the Western Partisans, led by Sonis; at Le Mans, the recapture of Auvours by General Gougeard's division; the storming of the Arcey position at Villersexel; the capture, near Paris, of Le Bourget by the *Francs-Tireurs de la Presse*; the attack on Coeuilly and Villiers by the 1st and 2nd Corps and on Stains by the 13th Battalion of the *Mobiles* of the Seine—exploits such as these bear witness to the spirit of the young soldiers. Unfortunately they lacked co-ordination.

As the battle progressed, so confusion became worse confounded. Units lost their sense of direction, became mixed up and finally disintegrated. A few groups, inspired by the example of their officers, continued here and there to perform prodigies of valour. But these unrelated episodes were no substitute for co-ordinated action, which, henceforward, was entirely lacking. If, overwhelmed by numbers or taken unawares by the first onslaught, the enemy abandoned the field of battle, as they did at Coulmiers, Bapaume, and Villersexel, the French troops managed to re-group, though they were incapable of taking up the pursuit. But if, as at Orleans, Le Mans or on the Lisaine, the battle continued for several days, these confused, fluctuating masses of men, helpless with exhaustion, fell into hopeless disorder. Whole units were seized with panic, the Breton *Mobilisés* at Le Mans, for example. To avert disaster, orders had to be given for the retreat, an operation which was executed in the greatest disorder, without halts for food, over roads rendered impassable by the winter. When the government of Paris was obliged by famine to conclude an armistice, the Armies of the Loire, of the East and of the North were in such a state of discouragement and wretchedness that it was a long time before they could again be led into battle.

For want of preparedness France found herself successively reduced, first to an army which, though of excellent quality, was inferior both in numbers and equipment, commanded by courageous leaders who were overwhelmed by adverse circumstances, and subsequently to great unco-ordinated masses, operating in haste and disorder.

In this war with no redeeming features France lacked neither men (for she raised 1,900,000 against the Germans' 1,300,000) nor arms (for the total number of rifles issued to the French troops exceeded that of the German Dreyse rifles, while the number of field-guns used by the French was 3,000 against 2,000 employed by the enemy). The French army did not lack courage: there was abundant proof of its military qualities. Nor was France sparing of her sacrifices: whereas the enemy lost 165,000 men killed and wounded, France lost 280,000. In addition, she suffered grievous losses of territory, treasure, and prestige. Such were the bitter, bloody fruits of a misconceived ideology combined with neglect.

The bolder one's plans, the greater must be one's strength; neither chance nor ready-made formulae can be relied upon as substitutes for preparedness; high stakes presuppose adequate resources. These inflexible rules apply to nations no less than to individuals, nor can the righteousness of one's cause or the nobility of one's principles make them any the less inexorable. But why is it only through the tears of the vanquished that this truth can be discerned?

BETWEEN TWO WARS

I

AN IMMENSE DISASTER, FOLLOWED BY A PEACE OF DESPAIR, SUFFERINGS WITH NO compensating rewards, a state with no foundations, with no army save the remnants returning from the enemy's prison-camps, a crushing indemnity, a quarter of the country occupied by the enemy, bloody civil war raging in the capital, while Europe looked on coldly or disdainfully: such were the conditions in which a vanquished France began anew to work out her destiny.

It might have been thought that these overwhelming misfortunes would have left France crushed for ever. Many there were who, hearing the crackle of rifles from the firing-squads in the Père-Lachaise, seeing the Tuileries Palace in flames, and thinking of the twelve régimes which had been overthrown in one lifetime, predicted the end of France. But they failed to take into account that inward power which has always enabled France to emerge from the valley of the shadow. In fact, the country was to make a rapid recovery—not, however, without paying the price of defeat. France was like the warrior returning to the fray, still bearing the arrow in his flesh.

As soon as the Treaty of Frankfort had been signed and the Paris rising crushed, the National Assembly undertook the task of restoring the country's military power, even before dealing with the question of the Constitution. This great legislative task was performed in an atmosphere of national unity and determination. "In framing this law," declared Gambetta, "we must heed nothing save the national interest", while General Billot recognized the fact that "not one word of politics has been pronounced in the debates of our Commission". "Great disasters," declared the secretary amidst the emotion of the whole Assembly, "bring with them great lessons. Wisdom consists in understanding them, and courage in profiting by them."

The laws of 1872, 1873 and 1875, dealing respectively with recruiting, organization and the constitution of cadres, endowed the army with foundations which were maintained up to the Great War: universal military service, the responsibility for defence being that of the whole nation; a regular army, constituting a permanent force; a vast system of military instruction, and, finally, a cadre for reserves liable to be called up in case of emergency. For, on the morrow of a struggle in which France was first invaded for want of numbers to throw against a numerically stronger enemy, and then defeated for want of cohesion in her belated levies, no one denied the necessity of organizing the masses of the nation, or of providing them with a backbone of well-trained regulars. Besides, was this not the system to which Prussia owed her triumph? The example of the victors was held to be a decisive argument. Though many found that Renan went too far in humility when he declared that "Germany's victory was a victory of knowledge and reason", the fact remains that, in the military as in other spheres, the French mind was to be influenced for many years by German thought.

The legislators were not, however, so slavish in their imitation as to abolish with one stroke of the pen the system of long-term military service which had been in use for sixty years. If a few innovators would have willingly made a clean sweep of the past, the politicians were more cautious. Thiers, whose long experience as a statesman had given him a deep insight into military philosophy, was averse from anything revolutionary. He was well aware that the old army had great qualities and strength. He continued to put his trust in the veterans' sense of duty rather than in a people's army. In any case, on the morrow of the Commune, while the new régime was still in its infancy, the future seemed to him to be too uncertain for the nation to be deprived of a powerful regular army. Moreover, the Ministers of War, Le Flô, Cissey, du Barail, and the generals in the National Assembly, which looked to them for guidance in military affairs, were not capable of renouncing their long-standing convictions overnight. Thanks to a long career among professional soldiers, and to a rich store of memories of Africa, the Crimea, and Italy rendered still more precious and poignant by defeat, these men were anxious to preserve in its essentials a system which they had known and tested. Speaking for the Army Commission, the secretary claimed that the law on recruiting "carefully preserved whatever could be preserved of existing legislation". Following the example of Niel's Act of 1868, the period of service was fixed in theory at five years, and it was expressly stated that no one was exempt in principle from the obligation of military service.

Democracy, however, had not yet permeated custom deeply enough to ensure that the law applied in practice equally to all. Although since 1848 the bourgeoisie had lost its electoral privileges, it still retained its privileged position by virtue of wealth, education, and local influence. The Assembly was acutely aware of what it owed to the "notables" and the "professors". The result was that young men with university degrees did no more than one year in the army, while members of the teaching profession and the Church were exempted altogether. And finally, since it was accepted that France should have no more and no fewer soldiers than Germany, where three classes only had been called to the colours, France kept her effectives down to the same level by exempting men who had a family to support and by freeing after six months' service those conscripts who drew a lucky number. The net result was that the long-term period applied to half the total contingent at most.

The legislators were again guided by the German example in the matter of the reserve. Up to the age of twenty-nine a man was considered as a reservist for the regular army. From twenty-nine to forty, he formed part of the territorial army and then of its reserve, bodies corresponding to the *Landwehr* and the *Landsturm* respectively. Eighteen and later nineteen army corps, each assigned to one particular region and established, even in peacetime, with their troops and supplies—the disorder caused in 1870 by the improvisation of big units was still remembered—were to be put on a war footing by incorporating in them 400,000 reservists. These corps would form the army in the field. The task of the Territorials would be to garrison the fortified towns, guard communications, and to man posts and provide working-parties behind the lines and in the interior.

The Act of 1889 brought no essential change in the system of defence. Although, following the general tendency of "lightening the burden", the theoretical period of service was reduced from five years to three, in practice, owing partly to the glut of recruits and partly to budgetary considerations, men had been freed after a period of forty months' service. Then again, the democratic swing had resulted in the abolition of certain exemptions, so that the "fighting parson" became a reality. But a good third of each class, including the students, were required to do one year at most. "It is a question of maintaining a high standard of culture in art, science and industry," said Berthelot. Meanwhile, the age limit was raised to forty-five, and the increase in the number of reserves made it possible for Freycinet, as Minister of War, to organize supplementary units, "mixed" and, later, "A" regiments. Nevertheless, the backbone of the first-line troops continued to be provided by the regular army.

With all that, the burden was heavy enough, especially for Frenchmen who, as individualists, take unkindly to military constraint. Every year 250,000 young men pass without transition from life in field, factory, or office to a monotonous existence in barracks. Somewhat intimidated on their arrival and anxious to do their best, they are astonished to find their older comrades helpful, their beds comfortable, and the food eatable.

Soon they are entirely caught up in the military machine. Their course begins with its "parades" on foot or on horseback, exercises, firing, lectures, lessons in the gymnasium or the riding-school. In the autumn rain or the winter cold the recruits grimly learn to handle their weapons, carry their packs, or ride their horses. In spring their horizon begins to widen somewhat, with longer marches and exercises in more varied country. With summer come route marches, camp, manœuvres which, though strenuous, are not without interest. In the intervals, there are everlasting reviews and inspections; there are arms, equipment, and tools to be cleaned, horses to be fed and groomed, guards and a thousand-and-one fatigues to be done. Dressed (rather shabbily) in uniform, subjected to strict discipline, the soldier, a Jack of all sorts of unexciting trades, pays the penalty of being no more than an anonymous cog in a gigantic collective machine. He reacts to it all with his characteristic unconcern. True, there are compensations. He is admired by the public when he marches along the esplanade or saunters through the streets of the town, looking starched rather than martial in his ungainly attire: long greatcoat, heavy boots, képi adorned with a tuft, and floss-silk gloves. True to his race, he appreciates the picturesque, unforeseen, exciting side of army life; he sings on the march, is keen on the range, throws out his chest during the march past and charges with deafening shouts. Nevertheless, he counts the days, believing, in his innocence, that his discharge means liberty.

These soldiers of the Third Republic, although somewhat independent, were full of goodwill and keen when the effort demanded of them was great, but careless about detail. They were highly susceptible to the example of their leaders, whose value was that of their cadres. Thanks to the impetus of defeat, these officers showed exceptionally high qualities. Those who had taken part in the recent battles had kept, together with their sorrow, such a firm determination to wipe out their disgrace that they were able to imbue their successors with the same high resolve. This resulted in a spirit of self-sacrifice which, despite some backsliding, remained a living force in the army up to the first World War. The new generation of young men demanded the honour of serving their country. Candidates for Saint-Cyr increased in numbers and quality. The majority of Polytechnicians chose a military career. New schools, such as Saint Maixent, Saumur, Fontainebleau and Versailles, entrance to which was by competitive examination, raised the standard of subalterns from the ranks. In the Army List the greatest names in France rubbed shoulders with the humblest, a circumstance which gave the army a higher average of ability and brilliance than was attained, perhaps, by any other social category. Under the prick of misfortune the army acquired a taste for work, which it had lacked for so long. Gradually the bad old traditions of the café, the contempt for books, the vacuous leisure, which had done so much to corrupt garrison life, gave way to something more worthy.

The growing complexity of training and administration added considerably to the officer's work. Every day he had to spend hours on the parade ground, training recruits, n.c.o.s and specialists; he had to lead his men on the march, ride, and concern himself with food, equipment and servicing of weapons and material. Then there were all the drills and special tasks inseparable from the community life of the army. But he loved his trade and enjoyed the privileges of action and authority which it comported. Though pay was low, the officer enjoyed a certain social distinction. He was respected in his garrison town. The tradesmen trusted him. He was the centre of attraction at social functions. His smartness was admired, and he was a favourite with women. He represented a desirable son-in-law, being a man of honour "who had prospects", or, in any case, a regular salary, to be followed, later on, by a pension.

To have officers of quality, however, is not enough. The lessons of 1870 showed that modern warfare demands of commanders both knowledge and method, for without these nothing is safe, not even honour. The old General Staff had contained a wealth of intelligence and experience. But, owing to its remoteness from the troops and to the fact that it was badly employed, its efficiency was mediocre in time of war. The army reformers took the course of disbanding it. Henceforth officers received their training in handling big formations not in the old school in the Rue de Grenelle, but in the Staff College, founded in 1875, and directed by Lewal. Its influence was to make itself felt throughout the army. It is true that it tended to the dogmatism which is inherent in scholastic theories and is exaggerated by the authoritarian tendencies of the army. Its claim to base a "doctrine" on the analysis of past events was to a great extent arbitrary, for the interpretation of history and the value of action are both dependent on non-recurring contingencies. Again, despite the obligation of Staff College graduates to return at intervals to their regiments, there was a considerable overcrowding of talent in the watertight compartments of the General Staff. Nevertheless, taken all in all, the Staff College was to endow the command with soundly trained officers, and to foster those high intellectual attainments without which the advanced principles of the art of war will remain a closed book to military leaders.

Moreover, this passion for learning spread throughout the whole army. Gone were the days when Ardent du Picq had to abandon the publication of his *Studies in War*, when Trochu aroused the angry astonishment of the High Command by the publication of some observations on military institutions, or when MacMahon declared: "I shall remove from the promotion list any officer whose name I have read on the cover of a book." Thanks to the work of men like Cardot, Maillard, Gibert, Grouard, Bonnal, continued by Négrier, Langlois, Foch, Colin, Maud'huy, Montaigne, Mayer and countless others, the history of the campaigns of the Revolution and Empire, the events of recent wars, technical and tactical problems were enthusiastically studied and discussed by circles which went beyond the professional soldiers to include members of the general public. A host of reviews and papers specializing in military questions: *Revue d'Histoire, Progrès, Spectateur*, etc., articles in newspapers and periodicals, all bear witness to the extent and quality of this intellectual movement and to the interest the subject aroused in the most varied quarters.

The intellect reigned supreme. The French army, open to every intellectual movement, outdistanced all other armies in the realm of armament. Shortly after the war the chassepot was replaced by the Gras rifle, with percussion fire on the centre of a metallic cartridge-case. Despite this change, and despite the new expense involved, in 1886 the Gras was scrapped in favour of the Lebel, which, thanks to its magazine, had a high rate of fire. Shortly afterwards the mounted troops were equipped with the magazine-loading carbine, and the revolver was put into service. The artillery underwent the greatest transformation of all. The excellent 80 and 90 mm. Bange field-pieces, the 120 and 155 mm. siege and fortress guns—robust, powerful, long-range weapons—marked the triumph of the removable breech invented by Reffye. With its sliding barrel, hydropneumatic brakes, and first-rate laying mechanism, this piece was unsurpassed in its day for regularity, rapidity, and precision of fire. Innovations and improvements were introduced in the whole range of engineering: for fieldworks, inter-communication, ballooning, bridging and demolitions. There was scarcely a tool, an ammunition wagon or boat for which a new model was not adopted between 1875 and 1900. At the same time Séré de Rivière undertook the tremendous task of organizing the defences of the country. On the northern and eastern frontiers, systems of fortifications—Dunkirk-Lille, Maubeuge-Mezières, Verdun-Toul, Epinal-Belfort—completed by barrier forts and duplicated by two groups of second-line defences—La Fère-Laon-Reims and Langres-Dijon-Besçanon—were designed to protect the territory outside the selected zones, purposely, in order to canalize the invasion. Paris was provided with a new ring of defensive works. In the Jura and the Alps enemy approach was barred by forts, Lyons serving as a redoubt in the defensive line of the mountains. And since the France of these days was in no mood for economies in the matter of precautionary measures, even her military ports were reorganized.

So heavy had been the cost of negligence that preparations against a new surprise were now completed down to the minutest detail. Under the inspiration of Miribel, the Army General Staff, a new institution in France, set to work to regulate in advance and in detail all the operations involved in a general mobilization. An *élite* of officers laboured in silence to organize its elements, to assign to each man his particular task, to amass, where they would be required, stocks of the arms, clothing, equipment, vehicles, supplies and munitions required by large masses of men, to work out their distribution and transport and to make provision for keeping them supplied. The whole scheme was worked out in tables, card-indexes and instructions which were distributed to everyone concerned, from the supreme commander down to the corporal of a squad, and kept constantly up to date. This was the Plan. It was a complicated document, concerning 4,000,000 men, 800,000 horses and 5,000,000 tons of supplies; it laid down regulations for railways, roads and stores, fixed itineraries, halts, billets, and sites. So minutely was every part of the machine designed that, if the occasion should arise, every single man would have his allotted place within it and would form a cog in its smooth-working mechanism.

But despite its exacting nature, this military activity had to function as it were in a vacuum, with a resulting sense of disillusion. Many a soldier with a very natural thirst for adventure was destined to reach the retiring age without ever having used a rifle or fired a gun except on the range. However, the most impatient among them found an outlet for their energy in the colonies. The desire for distant adventure, as old as the race itself, reappeared to offset the discontents of army life. France, consenting or not, played a leading part in the scramble for distant territories. Almost immediately after the close of hostilities French troops were called upon to put down the Kabyle revolt and to push forward their garrisons as far as the Algerian oases. Tunisia was occupied in 1881. The year 1885 saw the beginning of penetration into the interior of Senegal, the Niger and Dahomey. At the same time the Sahara was being opened up by a series of daring raids. By expeditions into the Congo basin and to the shores of Lake Chad, France achieved the conquest of immense new territories. This intense activity in Africa did not prevent her from marching into Tonkin in 1885 and wresting valuable concessions from China. Madagascar saw the arrival of French troops in 1895, and five years later a French corps occupied Pekin. Enterprising soldiers on the Moroccan frontier awaited the opportunity to invade the Sharef Empire.

From a tactical point of view, it is true, these expeditions were in a special class. Neither the enemy, the country, nor the material were comparable to those of a European war. No wonder that the "Metropolitan" school hastened to point out that the African army and the Colonial Infantry were losing their sound principles. Nevertheless, life in lonely outposts and desert columns taught the leaders to adapt themselves to circumstances. Manning a blockhouse on the slope of an isolated mountain, in the heart of some sandy plain or on the bank of some remote river, is an excellent training in initiative and energy. On the fringe of rebel-territory one must learn to gather information, to fortify one's position, to keep watch and to fight. In the wilds of Nature one must wage a constant struggle for existence, endure the most exhausting climatic conditions and overcome the terrors of solitude. A man's character, his eye for reality, his power of winning obedience—these things are tested to the utmost. He must wrest uncertain victory by forced marches across the worst that Africa or Asia can do in the way of broken country that offers ideal ambushes to his enemy. Hill crests taken by storm, stockades forced by a frontal attack, ambushes in deep ravines, gruelling climbs up rocky mountain sides, the anguish of desert solitude, death and suffering in the bush, the forest or the marsh, the biting cold of morning, the sweltering heat of noon and the terror that walks by night—these are some of the elements of which the Empire was built.

But public opinion viewed the development of colonial conquest with a critical eye. It is true that this demonstration of their country's undimmed martial valour provided balm for the nation's grief and support for its hopes. This yearning for glory serves to explain much of the reputation of men like Voyron, Négrier, Brière de l'Isle, Courbet, Duchêne and Archinard, and the popularity of others, like Rivière, Bobillot, Dominé, Borgnis-Desbordes, Lamy, Dodds, Marchand and Galliéni. As a pendant to the engraving of "Reichshoffen's Cuirassiers" every cottage had its coloured print representing the "Defence of Tuyen-Quan". Nevertheless, there was an element of reserve in the public's gratification. However cheaply these colonial expeditions were run, they were considered to be too costly. This accounted for the loss of life which later became another subject of popular dissatisfaction. "In every part of the world," declared the Radical Party's manifesto of 1885, "the government is playing fast and loose with the nation's wealth and the blood of her soldiers." There were other and more sinister doubts: "The colonies," said Paschal Grousset, "are a breeding-ground for pronunciamentos." But, above all, France turned her eyes towards the Vosges. Was it not an act of criminal folly to take troops away from the eastern frontier?

For, although desiring peace, the country indulged at the same time in hopes of revenge. It was more a question of dreams than of firm resolve; but by a process of wishful thinking, people came to believe that Right must triumph in its turn. The feeling grew that the defeat had been due to unfavourable circumstances. Those whose calling brought them into contact with the crowd—politicians, writers, professors, actors—had only to strike a certain chord to rouse their audiences. The verse of Déroulède, the songs of Paulus, and the novels of Erckmann-Chatrian enjoyed a tremendous vogue. Every schoolchild could recite the "Ballad of the Sword". There was hardly a public occasion, hardly a popular fête or a cabaret show at which there did not appear, amidst scenes of wild enthusiasm, the Alsatian girl with her big bow. The day when "the drums would beat" was awaited patiently but nevertheless ardently. No doubt remained that, sooner or later, "they" would give back Alsace and Lorraine. Any drawing-room or café pundit who prophesied that "war will break out in the spring of next year" was sure of an eager audience.

Then there were incidents enough to keep the Frenchman's defensive instincts keyed up. In 1875 Bismarck threatened to reopen hostilities. In 1887 the Schnoebele incident roused public opinion. In 1888 anxiety was felt by the accession of the young Wilhelm II. Right up to 1896 Crispi, feeling secure in his alliance with Berlin and Vienna, continued his provocations. The result was that the army became the object of a nation-wide cult. As a natural consequence, after the resignation of Thiers the Assembly elected a soldier as head of the executive. "Boulangism" was, at bottom, a manifestation of jingoism. People rushed out to see troops marching along the street; every head was bared, every eye was moist when the flag was carried past. The regimental band was always accompanied by a swarm of enthusiasts. On July 14 the whole population of every town turned out to cheer the garrison troops, while on the racecourse at Longchamps Paris gave a delirious welcome to 30,000 men marching behind their tattered standards.

II

However, as the years passed, the necessity for reconquering the lost provinces appeared less urgent. Circumstances in any case were unfavourable. Up to 1896 France was isolated in the presence of the Triple Alliance. By her subsequent treaty with Russia she undertook to respect the Treaty of Frankfort. But more important still was the fact that the relative power of France was steadily declining with the fall in her birth-rate. In 1871 there were as many Frenchmen as Germans. Twenty years later France had a population of thirty-eight millions compared with Germany's fifty millions. By the end of the next twenty years the population of France, which was more or less stationary, was less than two-thirds that of the Reich. A nation of "only sons" soon loses both the possibility and the desire for risky enterprises. Moreover, the country was divided by internal strife. The establishment of the Republic in a country in which great numbers remained attached to the past was not achieved without struggles which absorbed much precious energy and zeal. Public opinion in France was convulsed successively by the failure of the Restoration, the crisis of May 16, the Wilson scandal, the financial crash of *l'Union Générale*, the Panama scandal, the Boulanger fever, the anti-clerical war, and the storm of anti-Semitism. A people, humiliated by defeat and unnerved by polemics, seemed to have lost faith in itself. What was best in French thought turned away from national sources of inspiration. At the Sorbonne it was the philosophy of Kant, Fichte, Hegel, and Nietzsche that held the field. The more active exponents of social reform turned their backs on Fourier, Proudhon, Le Play, and Blanqui and marched behind the banner of Marx. This general sense of disillusion was reflected in the literature of the time, which fell back on symbolism, morbidity and exaggerated subtlety, or else wallowed in the mire by an excess of realism.

F

But these intellectual disturbances were accompanied by great material well-being. Like the Infanta weeping in the palace gardens, France in the nineties revelled in melancholy while enjoying the good things of life.

This contraction of the nation's ambitions was bound to have its effect on the military situation, and to make the obligation to serve in the army appear more onerous than ever. For one thing, military service had been extended in 1889 to include both the intellectual classes and the sons of wealthy families. Both these groups were keenly sensitive to the inevitable hardships of army life. As a consequence, a section of the intellectuals adopted towards the army an attitude of hostility, or, at least, of irony, which expressed itself in novels, pamphlets, songs and music-hall sketches. Not all, it is true, were as bitter in tone as *Sousoffs* or *Cavalier Miserey*, or as biting as *Colonel Ramollet*. But it became fashionable to hold up the army as a somewhat ridiculous institution in which Pitou, Lidoire, Dumanet, Bidouille or Chapuzot led their bewildered existence. A more serious tendency which revealed itself after the Boulanger episode was the distrust of the politicians for the "General Staff". Besides, armaments were costly, accounting for a third of the annual budget. In the end public opinion became exasperated at such lavish expenditure for a hypothetical situation which never materialized. The working-classes, who had increased both in numbers and cohesion with the development of industry, renounced the warlike sentimentality with which the Revolution had been tinged up to the Commune. A considerable section of the working-class adhered to the International, and recognized the existence of no enemies save those of the proletariat. In short, under many different forms France was witnessing the rise of anti-militarism.

Yet this criticism was for the most part superficial and showed no deep division of opinion. But then came the Dreyfus case. By some evil fate it happened that just as public sympathy was becoming estranged from the army a crisis arose which offered an ideal opportunity for uniting against it every shade of ill-will. Everything was present in this lamentable trial to poison public life and fan political passion: the plausibility of a miscarriage of justice, coupled with forgeries, manœuvres and abuses committed by the prosecution but indignantly rejected by those who, either by conviction or policy, wished to absolve from all blame the hierarchy whose lives were devoted to the defence of the country; an exasperating tangle of evidence with a thousand-and-one complicated incidents, intrigues, confessions, retractions, duels, suicides and subsidiary lawsuits in which the rival packs became befogged and infuriated; slanderous controversies exploited to the full by the press, by pamphlets and public speeches; an unhealthy frenzy engulfing, together with mutual forbearance, sincerity and friendship, every shred of elementary respect for the symbol of the nation's power around which Frenchmen had hitherto found it possible to unite. From that moment the generally accepted tendency towards strengthening the country's defences was reversed in favour of their reduction. Under the pressure of the illusions of pacifism and of the newly awakened distrust of the military mind, the army began to lose strength and cohesion. In July 1914 the Minister of War recognized the fact in these words: "At the beginning of the twentieth century the country allowed itself to be led astray by myths. It is an irrefutable fact that there has been a falling-off in its effort."

In the first place, effectives suffered a serious reduction. Whereas between 1875 and 1900, following increases in the German army, they had been raised from 450,000 men to 615,000, by the Act of 1905, which reduced the period of service in the regular army to two years, they dropped to 540,000, of whom 40,000 were non-combatant "auxiliaries". Against this must be set the abolition of exemptions and the resulting improvement in training. Another attempt to offset the reduction in the size of the nucleus of first-line troops was made by a better use of the reserve. Instead of ten classes as previously, thirteen classes of recruits were now attached to the active army. Each army corps would put into the field, besides its own formations, one supplementary division and two supplementary brigades. Every peacetime regiment was to have a supplementary cadre of officers on the active list who were assigned to their units in advance. Other measures, however, undid the good work of these arrangements. The two training periods of 28 days were reduced to 23 and 17 days respectively. In the same way, the territorials were to do 9 days instead of 13. Even then the call-out was subject to a series of crippling exceptions. Training periods were constantly reduced, postponed or cancelled altogether, to fit in with agricultural work, elections or personal convenience. In 1907, for example, thirty-six per cent of the total number of men nominally due failed to report. Moreover, the reserve, being composed of relatively old and less active men, should have been officered by exceptionally keen leaders. But in fact the supplementary cadres contained mostly elderly officers or men whose civilian employment kept them out of touch with their soldiers. And finally, there should have been a large number of camps in order to make the best use of the short periods available for training. This, however, was not the case. Up to 1912 there were only four big camps—at Châlons, Mailly, Coetquidan and La Courtine—whereas three times the number were needed.

This reduction in the number of first-line troops would have been relatively unimportant if armaments had been correspondingly increased. The scientific progress of the early twentieth century not only transformed industry but perfected the means of destruction. By exploiting to the full this increased industrial potential it would have been possible to counteract the disadvantages of inferior numbers. The period was marked by technical advances of all kinds: colloidal gunpowder gave increased explosive power to shells; a terrible weapon made its appearance in the new and simplified machine-gun; new processes of steel production made it possible to increase the calibre and range of field-guns without adding unduly to their weight; the telephone revolutionized intercommunications, the motor-car was becoming general, and the aeroplane was in the experimental stage. During the ten or fifteen years before the Great War, France, with her industrious population and her wealth of inventive genius and money, had the opportunity of recovering in the technical field the superiority which she was losing in numbers. But for that she would have had to make a decision in the political sphere. For it was only the government that, by providing credits, overcoming opposition to innovations and stimulating personnel, could create the necessary conditions for the reform of the army. In reality the government did little to encourage progress, and seemed at times ready to impede it.

In the first place, expenditure on armaments was severely limited. Between the years 1900 and 1912, out of a total war budget of twelve milliards of francs, nine hundred and fifty millions only were earmarked for new production, while Germany was spending approximately double this amount. There was the same unfortunate disproportion in the credits for military training. Year by year the services saw their allotments successively reduced, first by the Minister of War, who feared the criticism of his colleagues, then by the Treasury, and finally by the commissions of one parliamentary assembly or the other. And since it was considered impossible to reduce expenditure for personnel or maintenance, the economies were made at the expense of armaments. Three months before the mobilization, the War Budget was introduced to the Chamber of Deputies in these words: "In 1902 the services asked for 98,000,000 for the manufacture of new material; they received 49,000,000. In 1903 they asked for 59,000,000 and received 36. In 1906 they received 27,000,000 of the 44,000,000 asked." What is more, the services themselves, frightened by the opposition aroused by the so-called "death budgets", refrained from claiming the full amount of what they required, let alone from proposing the vast expansion which would have been necessary to ensure France's equality with, if not her superiority over, the armaments of her powerful neighbour.

Meanwhile the army itself showed little enthusiasm for the thoroughgoing reforms which the times demanded. This attitude was the more unfortunate in that it coincided with the adoption of tactical and strategical theories which postulated a superiority of material. The military authorities of the day, having had time during a prolonged period of peace to lose touch with the realities of war and to slip back into the academic habits of thought so dear to the French mind, "accepted no other theory of operations save that of the offensive", to quote the words used in Army Regulations of 1913. But since facts—and, above all, the fact of the enemy's fire—might conflict with the accepted theory, the authorities saw fit to admit the existence of moral factors, such as the will to win, which might after all be decisive. From this state of mind arose the tendency to neglect, or even to mistrust, weight of material, on the ground that the difficulties and delays occasioned by its deployment might hold up the speed of the attack on which alone, in accordance with the accepted theory, success depended. Pétain, who maintained that fire-power, since it is the factor that kills, should form the basis of every movement, was prevented from rising to the ranks of the higher command. Whereas Germany was equipping her army with a powerful heavy artillery, most of the French experts rejected outright any innovation of the kind. In 1909 the General Staff representative on the budget commission of the Chamber of Deputies expressed himself in these words: "You talk to us of heavy artillery. Thank God, we have none. The strength of the French army is in the lightness of its guns." To which the Minister of War added: "Quite useless. With a sufficient number of 75s we can smash any obstacle." This did not prevent the stock of shells, which experts, basing themselves on the experience of the Russo-Japanese war, advised should be 3,000 per 75 gun, from falling to 500 in 1906. When the decision was made, in 1910, to put the machine-gun into service, it was taken half-heartedly and unwillingly. "We have had some manufactured," said the Inspector-General of Infantry, "to satisfy public opinion. But this new weapon will not make the slightest difference to anything." It followed naturally that fortified places, being contrary to the offensive spirit, should be neglected. They were to be tolerated, as "maintenance depots", or as "pivots for manœuvre". Almost all the forts along the northern frontier, as well as the second-line forts built by Séré de Rivière, were either left as they were or abolished. Many officers were sceptical even of the possibilities of aviation, then in its infancy. On his return from a demonstration of military aircraft in 1910 the Commandant of the Staff College exclaimed: "The aeroplane is all very well as a sport. For the army it is useless"!

Nor did government policy tend to cultivate in the military leaders that optimism and self-confidence which would have favoured enterprise and initiative among them. After the Dreyfus case the authorities, on the pretext of ensuring the loyalty of the army, created trouble in its ranks. The spirit of self-sacrifice was undermined by a series of degradations, acts of favouritism, unjust denunciations or ridiculous exaggerations. The signs of the distress thus caused, however discreetly expressed among a body of men vowed to silence, were none the less revealing. The number of incidents into which the Minister of War was obliged to enquire—leaders with whom no one would shake hands, officers cold-shouldered, complaints, resignations, duels—was twelve times as great in 1904 as before. Between 1900 and 1911 the number of candidates for Saint-Cyr fell from 1,895 to 871, and for Saint-Maixent from 842 to 380, while the figures for re-enlisted n.c.o.s fell from 72,000 to 41,000. Every time-honoured guarantee for the promotion of officers and the choice of the commanders was violated. It is true that every peacetime period could provide examples of appointments which were nothing but a compromise between the claims of merit and of influence; but during the years preceding the Great War the abuse reached such proportions that on the outbreak of war half the generals had to be dismissed.

As was to be expected, the discipline and training of the troops suffered from the decline in the efficiency of their officers. In 1907, at Béziers, a whole regiment which had been called out to restore order in the streets threw down their arms and joined the rioters. Later on, the enforcement of the Three Years' Military Service Act gave rise to mutinies in several garrisons. The official report on the big 1913 manœuvres concluded with these words: "The troops are neither well trained nor disciplined.... The commissioned ranks showed a lack of experience which in a real campaign would have had disastrous consequences. ... The commanders do not carry out the missions with which they are entrusted with the vigour or the energy indispensable to success...." Conditions were such that the Commander-in-Chief, Brugère, gave up his post in 1901; one of his successors, Hagron, resigned in 1907, and his successor, Michel, followed suit on the same day. General Langlois, a capable and level-headed commander and a semi-official military expert, wrote on this occasion: "We owe the country the truth: the army is in a state of disorganization."

III

This slackening of effort in the French army meant a proportionate preponderance in German strength. For some time the Reich had shown no desire to crush France again, though it is true that the Iron Chancellor was so impressed by her rapid recovery that he contemplated launching an attack against her in 1875. But the crisis passed quickly. The pacific tendencies of the Republic, the Triple Alliance, and the understanding between Berlin on the one hand and the Tsar and England on the other made any French attempt at revenge less and less likely. Germany, moreover, was absorbed in a tremendous internal transformation. She had to get used to the idea of national unity and to the subordination of her age-old centrifugal tendencies to Prussian supremacy. At the same time, the development of her heavy industries caused an upheaval which shook up populations and interests, transferring part of the power of the Junkers to the progressive and liberal-minded business classes and driving the working-classes towards social democracy. And finally, the leaders of the Empire, William I, Bismarck, and Moltke, having grown old at their posts, were anxious to maintain unaltered the structure which they had built, rather than to run the risks inherent in new adventures. "I fear," said Bismarck, "that the German, that landlubber, will one day try to launch out on the water." In fact, up to the end of the nineteenth century, Germany was content to maintain the continental *status quo* and to keep her military forces on a level with those of France.

But with the German people, bursting with so many unfulfilled ambitions, moderation is never of long duration. With her birth-rate increasing by nearly a million per annum, her volume of industrial production quadrupled, that of her foreign trade tripled and her national wealth doubled between the years 1875 and 1905, with ten times the tonnage of shipping in her ports, and flourishing affairs in every part of the world, supported by capital investments and an indefatigable army of commercial travellers; with her spirit of discipline and gift for organization always and everywhere at work—Germany felt the balance of power tilt heavily to her advantage. Conscious of her progress and pressed by new needs, the Empire found her living-space too small. The "old gentlemen" who held the movement in check were disappearing one by one. William I and Frederick III died in 1888, soon to be followed by the nonagenarian Moltke. In 1890 the young Emperor, William II, dismissed Bismarck, and the way was clear for the *Weltpolitik* of a dynamic, expansionist, and conquering Germany.

But she had entered the race too late. Wherever German imperialism wished to expand it found the place occupied by others. A few colonies here and there in the Dark Continent, a base in China, one or two small Polynesian islands, facilities for building a railway in Asia Minor—these concessions seemed to her ridiculously inadequate compared with the advantages which England, France, Russia, and Belgium had secured for themselves while there was yet time. Nor was it easy to get the better of rivals who hampered her economic expansion by adapting their own production and adjusting tariffs so as to keep out goods "made in Germany". But this was not all. European states which had shown themselves on the whole quite favourable to the policy of Berlin so long as it consisted in maintaining the European system established by the defeat of France now began to feel alarm at Germany's ever-growing ambitions; hence a series of diplomatic understandings designed to redress the balance. The settlement, in 1904, of Franco-British disputes, the *rapprochement* in 1905 between Rome and Paris and the fact that Russia, after her defeat in Manchuria, was turning her attention to the Balkans and the Dardanelles, were so many obstacles to Germany's expansion.

Germany viewed these developments with irritation and alarm. Once more she vented her ill-humour on France. There were, it is true, counsellors who advised her to pick a quarrel with England, since "the future is on the sea", or to expand in the direction of Russia, whose Baltic, Polish, and Ukrainian marches offered tempting baits to the Prussian colonists, industrialists and bankers, just as formerly they had tempted the Teutonic Knights. Others favoured the *Drang nach Osten*, profiting by the dissensions between the peoples of the Balkans and the Danube basin and by the prostration of the Turks. But it would seem as though the path of history always leads the Teutons back to their "hereditary enemies", the Gauls. The French conquest of Morocco offered pretext enough, and although subsequently it was to be Austro-Russian hostility which came to the fore, it remained true that, in every crisis, France was the target at which Berlin was aiming.

This new phase of German policy demanded vast military preparations. The existence of the Franco-Russian alliance meant that the Empire had to be prepared to fight on two fronts and to ensure that her enemies were powerless to strike their main blows simultaneously. Everything else, therefore, had to be subordinated to the necessity of crushing France in the shortest possible time. In 1905, Schlieffen, rejecting the ideas of Moltke, perfected his plan for an offensive which aimed at dealing France the knock-out blow by a vast outflankin movement through Belgium. An undertaking of this scope, however, entailed the immediate engagement of numerically strong formations, capable of moving swiftly—("Strengthen that right flank!" cried Schlieffen on his deathbed)—as well as the employment of material heavy enough to smash the obstacle formed by the Belgian and French forts at the very outset of the campaign. At the same time his theory of warfare, like that put forward by Bernhardi in *The Next War*, was that strategy, sparing neither persons nor property, should set out to shorten resistance by deliberately making the coming war as terrible and as ruthless as possible.

Ever since 1892 Germany had the the system of two years' military service, except in the cavalry, where the period was three years. But the contingents were so strong numerically that only half the available number of men was incorporated. It was possible, therefore, to swell the permanent establishment by merely abolishing certain categories of exemptions. This was the intention underlying the Acts of 1912 and 1913 by which the German army was increased to 850,000 men. It was equally simple, thanks to the wealth of man-power, to form reserves of young, picked soldiers. The whole body was provided with a strong cadre of 150,000 regular n.c.o.s As for armaments, the expenditure earmarked for new material, which, up to 1904, did not exceed an average of

100,000,000 marks per annum, increased to 160,000,000 for the years 1905–6–7, reaching an annual total of 200,000,000 up to 1912, and, finally, of 430,000,000 in each of the Budgets of 1913 and 1914. As a consequence, the army was equipped with the most powerful and modern material.

There was a certain amount of opposition to the increased expenditure. In the Reichstag, the veteran deputy Bebel protested on behalf of the Social Democrats. Tirpitz and the advocates of a big navy policy considered that such lavish expenditure on land forces would have been better directed to building battleships. Even in the army the "quality before quantity" school of thought, backing the shade of Frederick the Great against that of Scharnhorst, maintained through their mouthpiece Von der Goltz that it would be preferable to provide the Reich with a smaller army, but one superior in quality, armaments, and training. But all these discordant voices were drowned in the shouts of approval from the enthusiastic majority. In the spring of 1914 Germany could put into the field twenty-five regular army corps, in addition to eleven cavalry divisions, and was able to organize twenty-eight reserve divisions of first-line quality. The whole formed an army such as the world had never seen before. It was accepted by everybody as a matter of course that in the next war, whatever the pretext might be, the mighty torrent would sweep, in the first place, towards Paris.

Meanwhile the tumult gradually awakened France from her slumbers. A succession of incidents from 1905 onwards convinced her that the chances of continued peace were small indeed. William II's visit to Tangiers, the Algeciras Conference, the Casablanca incident of the deserters from the Foreign Legion, the appearance of the "Panther" at Agadir, the sharp negotiations on the question of the Congo-Cameroons frontier, the defeat of the Turks by the Balkan States, followed by that of Bulgaria by her former allies—all these successive events made public opinion aware of a complex of obscure tendencies which the ancients would have called Fate, Bossuet the finger of God, and Darwin the law of the species, the result of which was to drag Europe into the abyss of war. True, there were highly placed individuals who, appealing to reason or allowing themselves to be swayed by sentiment, refused to believe in the imminence of danger. "There will be no war!" declared General Brun, the Minister of War in 1910. In 1912, when Driant, in the Chamber of Deputies, exposed German preparations for war, he was met with a cry from Marcel Sembat of "No, no! Not *that*!" On July 31, 1914, Briand declared, with a shrug of his shoulders: "I know the Germans, and they are not mad. They won't go to war." But even those who were responsible for these sallies were nevertheless anxious. Brun made an increase of one third in the artillery. In his book entitled *Make a King or Else Make Peace*, Sembat described the looming threat. As Prime Minister, Briand sponsored the bill for three-years' military service. Beneath all the doctrines and attitudes and prejudices lay an instinctive realization of the facts. There was the political evolution of leaders like Millerand and Viviani, and the rise in the popularity of Poincaré, the trustee of France's watchfulness. There was the diplomatic activity of ambassadors like the brothers Cambon, Delcassé, Barrère, and Paléologue. In the realm of the mind, men like Boutroux and Bergson gave new life to the spiritual side of French thought, while Péguy and Barrès appealed to the precocious maturity of a young generation who sensed the presence of the Gleaner. And so there arose among an *élite* a consciousness of their imperishable national inheritance, a renaissance which a contemporary can only sketch in its rough outlines, but which History will limn in every detail.

This change in public opinion had its effect on the relationship between the politicians and the military. The indifference, if not the ill-will, shown hitherto by the Government in its dealings with the army soon gave way to solicitude. In 1910, 1911, and 1912 reforms in cadres and promotions were incorporated successively in acts affecting the artillery, the infantry and the cavalry. Another Act of Parliament put an end to the decline in the corps of professional n.c.o.s by introducing radical reforms in their living conditions, pensions and prospects of employment in state services. In 1913 pay increases were introduced for all ranks. At the same time it began to be part of official policy to show the troops, who for some years had been hidden from the public eye. There were brilliant parades everywhere. In 1912, on the parade-ground at Vincennes, Paris inaugurated its short-lived series of spring reviews. Every garrison town had its Saturday night torchlight tattoo when the public could indulge its enthusiasm for stirring military marches. The penetration of Morocco, begun in 1908, received a new impetus, and it was to Lyautey, a soldier, that full powers for the administration of the conquered territory were entrusted. Finally, in 1911, the Commander-in-Chief in the person of General Joffre, who, up to that time had been pushed aside, became responsible in great part for the preparation of the army which he would have to lead. Henceforward, no action was taken in the matter of organization, armament and training save on his recommendation. From that moment, despite the fact that France had, up to the war, six ministers in three years, the army enjoyed the benefits of continuity in the controlling authority.

But in order to attain parity with the German forces, France had at all costs to increase the numerical strength of her army. Thanks to the Acts of 1912 and 1913, the army of the Reich outnumbered that of France by over 30 per cent. With two classes called to the colours France would have had 540,000 men and Germany 850,000. Thus, after 60 years of a seriously declining birth-rate, a nation which formerly had been so prolific as to be prodigal with the lives of her soldiers saw herself faced with the agonizing problem of numbers. There were schemes for palliatives which, given a long-term policy, might have achieved some measure of success, but as a consequence of a lack of forethought the country had to fall back on emergency measures, that is, the most costly of all. As early as 1901 Messimy had pointed out the advantages, especially for the provision of covering troops, of forming specialized units which would be used with the masses of conscripts. But it was too late to introduce a reform of this nature. Moreover, the technical reasons for the formation of such special formations in order to obtain the maximum efficiency in the use of certain modern weapons were not conclusive at a time when each separate element of the army was identical and interchangeable, and armed with one single pattern of rifle and a single type of cannon. Mangin published his views on the contribution to the defence of the home country which could be made by "the black force". However, the peculiar difficulties inherent in the recruitment and use of black troops involved a delay which precluded any early results from their incorporation. Jaurès, in his *New Army*, published in 1910, maintained that the militia, bringing to bear the strength of the whole nation at one and the same time, would, in the long run, prove invincible. But, even admitting that the system of the nation in arms would have produced the required number of soldiers, it remained true that, faced with a skilful enemy, intent on *Blitzkrieg* methods, these large masses of men would have to be sufficiently trained and organized to be thrown into battle immediately. In short, the only possble solution capable of being immediately applied was, in 1913, the system of three years' military service. This drastic measure raised the establishment of the regular army to 750,000, put the corps of four frontier provinces on a permanent war footing, and only reduced by one-third the proportion of reservists necessary to mobilize all the first-line troops. But it was an emergency measure, laying an almost unbearable burden on the youth of the country, with the risk of impeding seriously the education of the student class; a measure which could not possibly have been maintained for any length of time. In fact, scarcely had the law been promulgated than it was violently attacked. Nevertheless, it achieved its object; when the Austrian Archduke fell to the assassin's bullet, France had three classes under arms.

But although it is possible to mobilize troops by what amounts to makeshift measures, it is quite another story when it comes to providing them with the necessary equipment. Progress was impeded by the enormous expense involved, by the inherent difficulties of planning and manufacture, and by the dilatory procedure usual in the technical services. After the 1905 scare, it is true, 200,000,000 francs had been earmarked for the purpose, over and above the expenditure provided in the Budget; but this sum had only barely sufficed to make good the deficiencies in military stocks. And although the annual credits for armaments and equipment rose from 92,000,000 for the period 1905 to 1910 to 240,000,000 for the period 1911 to 1914, the Germans were spending double that amount. In 1913 the government asked for an exceptional credit of 1,410,000,000 francs in order to make up the leeway; but the bill, after a long series of amendments, was only finally passed by the Senate on July 14, 1914.

This combination of routine in the technical sphere and short-sightedness in the political had as its result a serious inferiority in material. Despite the fact that the number of machine-guns allotted to the infantry had been doubled in three years, France at the beginning of the war could put only 2,500 automatic weapons into the line against the enemy's 4,500; and although, as compared with the year 1909, the artillery had been increased by 33 per cent, yet against the French army's 3,800 75 mm. guns, capable of firing 1,300 rounds, the enemy could put 6,000 77 mm. cannon firing 2,000 shells each. More important still, each German army corps had 52 howitzers, 36 of 150 mm. and 16 of 150 mm., whereas the French army corps possessed none at all. Moreover, the German artillery comprised in addition 210 mm. howitzers and long-barrelled field-pieces of 100 and 130 mm., all modern, and with a range of 4, 7 and 9 miles respectively, whereas, apart from a few 155 mm. "Rimailhos", the French had nothing but the old 120 mm. "Baquets", made 30 years earlier for use in the forts. These were slow-firing, short-ranged guns, extremely difficult to move. On January 6, 1914, the Inspector-General wrote: "As for siege and garrison artillery, nothing has been done for the last 40 years"; and, in point of fact, France could boast of nothing more modern in this category than the 270 mm. mortar, dating back to 1875, which could hurl a 150 kilo. shell over a distance of 3 miles, while on the other side of the Rhine they had brand-new mortars of 280 mm. calibre firing 340 kilo. shells over a distance of 6 miles, and were secretly preparing the famous 420 mm. As far as aviation was concerned, France since 1910 had made great strides in a field where her national inventiveness, supported by public opinion, gave her a considerable initial advantage. Despite this, in July 1914 France possessed no more than 136 aeroplanes to Germany's 220. With lighter-than-air machines the relative situation was still more unfavourable for France; without mentioning the Zeppelin, vastly superior to the old-fashioned dirigible still in use in the French army, the German "Drachen" were better than anything the French possessed in spherical balloons. The commissions entrusted with settling these multifarious details—unimportant in themselves, but important, when added together, in influencing the outcome of a battle—deliberated endlessly without coming to any conclusions. And whereas her potential enemy adopted the field-grey uniform and practical equipment, made use of field-kitchens, and provided his troops with up-to-date material for intercommunications and observation, the French troops kept to their red trousers and knapsack dating from the Second Empire, cooked their rations in mess-tins and used primitive telephones and an insufficient number of secondrate field-glasses. In brief, when the hour of battle struck, the German army was prepared to fire, at a greater distance and with greater ease, twice the amount of lead as its opponent.

Nevertheless, when France was compelled to unsheathe the sword, her enemy discovered that it was not in vain that, during forty-three years of peace, she had claimed thirty million years out of the lives of her sons, spent eighty milliards of gold francs on armaments, and preserved among her officers sufficient of the military virtues to enable them to lead a nation to war. It is true that the first battle was to demonstrate that lack of material, mistakes in strategy and tactics, are paid for in soldiers' lives, in ruin and destruction; but it became clear at the same time that all the preparations made during the long truce had their meaning and their value. Those useless regiments, those silent guns and sleeping forts, those commanders turned office-workers, those long years of inglorious frustration, those conventional exercises, fatigues and lectures became overnight the only arguments that mattered in the court of War, that heartless, though by no means unjust judge.

THE GREAT WAR

THE GREAT WAR WAS A REVELATION. NO SOONER HAD THE WHITE POSTERS BEARING the mobilization order appeared on the walls before 4,000,000 men, a quarter of the active population, left their farms, their factories or their offices. A further 4,000,000 were to follow. Another 5,000,000 men and women were absorbed by industry and public services. War laid hold not only on individuals but on the nation's business life. Half the national wealth—a hundred milliards of gold francs—was swallowed up in its maw. By this fact alone the system on which world economy reposed was turned upside down. Liberty of production and distribution were things of the past; so were stability, social classes, and personal fortunes. Elections were suspended, opinion was watched, the press censored. All men's thoughts, desires, and interests became focused upon the same grim, haunting drama.

Like others before it, this revolution was but the culmination of long years of change, suddenly brought to a head by the cataclysm. For generations universal suffrage, compulsory education, the equality of rights and obligations had combined to mould the nation into a single whole. Local characteristics had been blurred by industrialization and city life. The mechanical age provided everyone with mass-produced goods. People's minds had been directed by the press to the same topics. Men's interests had extended to wherever their property might be. Political parties, trade unions, and sport all fostered the collective spirit. Transportation, travel, and public hygiene accustomed people to a host of communal controls. In short, the uniformity, the bustle, the mass movements and mechanization to which men and women were subjected by modern life had preconditioned them for mass mobilization and for the brutal, sudden shocks which characterized the war of peoples.

France then, had only to draw her sword to unite all her children in a common fervour, animating not only the mass but also the individual. Inspired by patriotism, religious faith, hope, or hatred of the foe, he was both ready and willing to be torn from home and family. Theories, on the other hand, which had been considered to be potential obstacles to the war effort, vanished into thin air. Not one organized group raised its voice to condemn mobilization. Not one trade union thought for a moment of hindering it by strikes. In Parliament, not one vote was cast against the war estimates. The number of deserters, which had been officially estimated beforehand at 13 per cent, proved in the event to be less than 1.5 per cent of those called to the colours, while the recruiting offices were besieged by 350,000 volunteers. Frenchmen living abroad flocked back by train and ship to the mother country. The suspects, whose names appeared on "List B", begged to be sent to the front. Three thousand peacetime deserters returned from abroad to crave the honour of being allowed to fight.

Surrounded as he was by an atmosphere of general consent, the conscript joined up willingly. The last thing in the world that he wanted was to appear lacking in courage. Recruiting, moreover, was by districts. This had the advantage of fostering a man's self-respect, of making it possible for him to travel with lads from his own village and to find friends among the crowd. In any case, this mass mobilization was carried out in perfect order. The recall of men on leave, the call-up of reservists of covering units, the taking over of the railways by the military authorities, the placing of guards along lines of communication, the general mobilization of men, horses, vehicles and the requisitioning of supplies, presented a vast and spectacular operation which inspired widespread optimism and obedience. Out of 25,000 trains set in motion during the first few days of mobilization, only 19 were late.

Scarcely had he reached his depot before each man was absorbed in a host of preparations. Signed-on, dressed, armed, equipped, inspected, he became a cog in the machine. When the day of departure arrived, surrounded by his pals in the ranks, under the eye of the officers who were to lead him, he derived satisfaction in maintaining the silence imposed on him, in falling-in correctly and standing smartly to attention. A little foot-and-arms drill gave the men the feeling of their collective power. At last everything was ready. The time had come. There were peremptory orders. Then, sustained by the salutary rigour of military discipline, the soldier marched off with a confident step to meet his destiny.

The first encounter with the enemy was a tremendous surprise. The whole French strategic plan was upset by the enemy's vast enveloping movement and by his use of his reserves. On the tactical plane, the revelation of the enemy's fire-power made nonsense of the accepted theories. Morally, the illusions behind which the soldiers had taken refuge were swept away in a trice.

The whole army was taken unawares. Between August 20 and 23, 1914, it passed without transition from a sense of absolute security to the realization of its dire peril. Some units, it is true, cavalry or covering troops, had been under fire before, but only in isolated incidents. Suddenly, at one blow, from the Upper Rhine to the Sambre, 1,200,000 Frenchmen went into battle.

From that moment the French commander's initial conception had to undergo radical changes. Whereas the original intention had been to seize the initiative by moving across from west to east at least four of his armies, three of them had had to be sent north in haste. The decision was to be fought out, not in Lorraine, as had been anticipated, but in Belgium. Moreover, in order to operate as a single unit, the French had deliberately allowed the Belgian army to be neutralized. Seventy-four French divisions of cavalry and infantry had gone forward on the same day. Irrespective of whether they were to be engaged in the Vosges mountains, the Lorraine plateau, the Meuse district, the Ardennes forest or the Charleroi plain, every one had received the same order, namely, "To advance and press back the enemy wherever he is encountered."

The large units were in column formation. At first the troops might easily have been under the impression that they were engaged in an already familiar operation; there was the same order in ranks and files, the same picturesque appearance, the same minor discomforts of the march: the sun, the dust, the weight of the pack. Suddenly the distant growl of cannon produced an uneasy feeling that things were about to happen. Physical fatigue was accompanied by a gnawing anxiety as the unknown goal drew nearer. This feeling, however, was soon replaced by one of confidence, the result of willingness to do one's bit, combined with a certain curiosity.

Contact with the enemy came with brutal suddenness. The Germans, having been the first, strategically, to take the offensive, adopted defensive tactics for the first clash. They were already deployed before they advanced. The French spear-point met their "rake". Neither charges with fixed bayonets made to the sound of bugle-calls by a few tenacious sections nor heroic individual exploits were of any avail. It became evident from one moment to another that all the valour in the world is helpless against fire-power.

While the infantry was dashing forward to the attack, the artillery took up its position. With the best will in the world, the commanders needed time to choose their gun positions, to set up observation-points and organize liaisons. At what were they to fire, anyhow, when all that could be seen of the enemy was a few faint gleams of well-aligned cannon? If the infantry could indicate the targets which impeded their progress, the artillery would have been able to intervene with good effect. But how could these men, caught up in a hell of enemy fire three miles ahead of the batteries, send back the precise indications with sufficient speed? In many cases the artillery had not finished its preparations before the attack was broken. The bursts of gunfire from the French side could be no more than reprisals, too late and too little to change accomplished facts.

From his improvised observation-point the commander of the large unit observed the setback suffered by the first echelons. He still had his reserves, ready to be thrown in to force a decision. But so complete was the failure of his first attack that it gave him no indication of the best way to employ them. More often than not he used his available troops to "support the attack". It might, after all, be possible, it was argued on the principle of "mass multiplied by speed", to renew the forward movement.

While the fight raged in the forward areas, the reserves, waiting under some sort of cover, were a prey to the gloomiest forebodings. The punishment which they had to take without the possibility of retaliation, the gruesome tales of those returning from the front line, the sight of the wounded streaming back with bleeding bodies—these things depressed them all the more because they had to remain inactive. Morale was already low when the order came to advance, and was further shaken as the danger zone was reached. In many cases the troops were incapable of holding on under the hurricane of fire; they stopped and scattered at random until they became entangled with the first echelons which they were supposed to lead. There were even cases when, under the impact of some unexpected incident, the strain proved too great for their tightly stretched nerves. Panic swept through the ranks, which broke and fled. The collapse was of short duration and its effects rapidly localized. In any case, these incidents provided ample demonstration that to throw in more troops under the fire of an enemy force which has remained intact is merely to increase the total of killed.

Soon the exhausted troops, lacking any hold on the ground they occupied, had to be withdrawn. Along the whole line, whether pressed by the enemy or not, the men began their melancholy retreat. Subsequent reports and records might give to these chaotic movements some semblance of a logical *raison d'être*; but in the opinion of the soldiers who took part in them at the time, the whole operation was senseless and absurd.

This unfortunate beginning was immediately followed by a hasty retreat. A withdrawal in the northern sector exposed the country's vital industrial centres. In nine days France lost Lille, Roubaix, Tourcoing, Valenciennes, Cambrai, Arras, Saint-Quentin, Amiens, Charleville, Mézières, Rheims, Laon, and Soissons. Maubeuge capitulated, the Channel ports were threatened, coal mines, iron deposits, factories, wheat- and sugar beet-growing districts were abandoned. A sixth part of the population passed under the control of the enemy, the capital was endangered and the government displaced. If one large unit had collapsed, if one commander had lost his head or his men their nerve, disaster would have followed. Resistance would have been impossible north of the Loire, the British would have fallen back to their bases, the Belgians would have capitulated, and the German Emperor would have ridden as a conqueror under the Arc de Triomphe. Such is the weakness of France's northern frontier that one defeat there imperils the whole country.

Joffre saw the collapse of all his plans, the refutation of all his information and the invalidation of all his orders. On his staff maps at Vitry-le-François, at Bar-sur-Aube, at Romilly, the ever descending circles and arrows bore witness to the heavy blows to which his forces were subjected. He learned in quick succession of the setback in Alsace, the extension of the enemy's outflanking movement to the north of the Meuse, the presence in the front line of the German reserve corps, the failure of the offensives in Lorraine and the Ardennes and the withdrawal of Lanrezac and French, whose forces were outflanked after Charleroi. Every despatch-rider, every telephone message, every officer's report added to the dismal catalogue of reverses; the reserve units engaged on the Somme were incapable of carrying out the movements required of them; the government was demanding the despatch of three army corps for the defence of Paris; the battles of Tannenberg and the Masurian Lakes had put an end to Russian incursions into East Prussia; there was delay in the concentration of Maunoury's army; Maubeuge had capitulated; the British were accelerating their retreat; the attempt to regain positions on the Meuse had failed. A stand on the Aisne was impossible. Could one be made on the Marne? The censorship might conceal part of the truth from the public, the soldiers might be unaware of what was happening outside their own sector, opinion among the General Staff might adopt an attitude of professional optimism; but the Commander-in-Chief could harbour no illusions.

It was fortunate for France that Joffre, having begun badly, did not lose his head. At first he had put enough faith in certain preconceived doctrines to base his plan of campaign on them. But, having realized that the remedy depended upon himself alone, he threw over his theories and pitted the whole of his powerful personality against the course of events. Thanks to his common sense, his obstinacy, and his iron constitution, he was able to rise above disaster. On the very evening of Charleroi, his plan was made; he would strengthen his left flank at the expense of his right, avoiding battle until the operation was complete, and then launch an all-out attack along the whole line. He was determined, whatever the cost, to see the plan through. He sacrificed Mulhouse, withdrew troops from the forces in Lorraine, and risked the loss of Verdun. He was deaf to the apprehensions of the ministers and the fears of Paris. By plugging up gaps, eschewing local successes, and imposing his will, he maintained enough cohesion to enable his armies to turn round and strike all at the same time when the order was given.

The armies bent, but did not break. After leaving a third of their effectives on the battlefields of the frontier, retreating for ten nights and days, during which certain units covered two hundred and fifty miles, living amid the confusion of columns mixed up with civilian populations fleeing from their burning villages, they had remained both morally and physically sound. There were, it is true, shadows in the picture, the Commander-in-Chief was "informed that bands of retreating soldiers were committing acts of pillage and violence". He saw himself obliged to order that "the fugitives be pursued and shot". Most of the divisions of reserves showed a lack of cohesion. The Governor of Paris wrote to Joffre as follows: "Unless you send me first-line troops it is impossible for Paris to hold out." The commander of a group of territorial divisions considered them to be "poorly officered and of mediocre quality". Nevertheless, not a single column could be named which, from the Sambre to the Seine, failed to follow its prescribed itinerary. Despite the exhausting march with its fierce rearguard actions, and the counter-thrust at Guise, less than ten thousand unwounded prisoners—apart from captured garrisons and forts—fell into enemy hands. Nowhere was heard the cry of "Every man for himself", or "We are betrayed"—symptoms of a disorderly rout. In fact, the army pulled itself together quickly, conscious that it deserved something better than its present fate.

The German defeat was determined less by the development of the engagements themselves than by the surprise occasioned among the enemy by the French offensive. The outflanking of their wing on the River Ourcq by Maunoury, the advance of Franchet d'Espérey, followed by that of French, into the gap between the two German armies on the right, the resistance of Foch and Langle in Champagne, Sarrail's counter-attack in the direction of Verdun, and the recovery of Castelnau and Dubail at either end of the Charmes gap certainly put the Germans in an awkward strategical situation. But the cracks were repairable. In fact, they were made good before the withdrawal. Although in September, thanks to the experience they had gained, the French troops were fighting incomparably better than in August, they had nowhere gained tactical successes capable of breaking the enemy's resistance and putting him to flight. Again, the balance of forces had tipped in the Allies' favour since the Germans had sent two army corps and one cavalry division from the west to fight on the Russian front. However, the Germans still retained numerical superiority. On September 8 eighty French and British divisions faced eighty-one better-armed enemy divisions. On material grounds, therefore, there was no impelling reason for the enemy's retreat.

But the fact remains that he was taken by surprise. Whereas the Frenchman, once he has paid for his negligence, unexpectedly recovers from the blow, the German, unsurpassed in careful preparations, loses his wits when faced by an unforeseen situation. Such was the psychological aspect of the first phase of the war. Moreover, by a strange accident, while their troops showed themselves superbly disciplined, the generals of the Imperial Army were at loggerheads. A vicious system of command resulted in von Kluck's disobedience, Bülow's isolation, and the fact that the Crown Prince's forces were inordinately stretched. Remembering the victories of 1866 and 1870, when generals acted on their own initiative, each one of them claimed to act as he thought best. What is more, these disciples of Nietzsche admitted no restraints on their own powers. It might be thought that unity would have been imposed from above by a firm hand. Not at all. For, thanks to the superstitious belief in a great name—quite usual in victorious armies—the supreme authority had been vested in von Moltke, a man of refined and delicate mind but afflicted by a malignant disease and lacking the firmness by which a leader imposes his faith on others.

The spell was broken. For the first time for over a hundred years France had beaten Germany in a big-scale battle. Psychologically the game was won. From the moment the Imperial Armies had been forced to turn back, the poison of doubt began to circulate in their veins. Conversely, the confidence in their national might, which formerly had been second nature to Frenchmen, suddenly returned to them. Accepted calmly and without bombast, the victory united in a common pride a people long disunited by humiliation.

II

For over three years each of the opposing armies endeavoured to deal the other a mortal blow. But thanks to their approximate equality in numbers, material and valour, they remained rooted to the same positions. Every conceivable type of defences—trenches, dug-outs and pill-boxes—gave both sides a high capacity for resistance. In order to launch an attack it was necessary to amass a tremendous amount of material, to prepare to set in motion a vast and complicated mechanism, and subsequently to limit the offensive to a narrow front.

In the sector chosen for the attack the enemy positions were carefully studied, photographed and observed from the air, and reconnoitred by patrols. Thanks to these preliminary measures the commander was enabled to make his appreciation of the nature and weight of the material he required and to decide how it should be used. Then came the siting of the artillery. The batteries were placed at night and grouped according to their particular mission. Targets were indicated, zones of fire-action defined, and the necessary adjustments made. Stocks of ammunition began to pile up near the guns or in dumps.

During this time the infantry and sappers were busy with preparations for the attack, digging parallel and communication trenches, making roads and tracks, laying down narrow-gauge railways, preparing parks, dressing-stations and commanders' posts. Supplies were being brought up and distributed by large numbers of trains, lorries and trucks. The troops brought forward for the operation poured into their bivouacs. All this traffic had to be controlled and policed. A feverish but orderly activity involved every one and everything.

Suddenly the artillery opens up. Every type of instrument plays its part in this orchestra. Light and medium guns pound the trenches and blast gaps in the network. Short-barrelled, high-trajectory pieces of great calibre are given the task of destroying flanking defences, penetrating dug-outs and bombarding strong-points. Long-range artillery endeavours to neutralize the enemy batteries, to paralyse communications by keeping roads, bridges and cross-roads under fire, and by shelling cantonments, bivouacs and railheads.

While the artillery is doing its work, the infantry is putting the finishing touches to its preparations for the attack, and receiving the last items of equipment—cartridges, grenades, rations, tools and explosives. The officers go out on reconnaissance and return with serious, drawn faces. The private soldier scribbles a few awkward lines to the people at home—often the last he will write.

At nightfall the troops move off, heavily loaded and heavy-hearted, but resigned to go through with the job, thanks to the discipline of their long training. The road along which they march, with its stream of convoys, the newly made track into which they branch, the narrow-gauge railway which they cross and the artillery lines which they can see on their way—all bear witness to the existence of an ever-watchful and ever-present authority.

Before reaching the danger-zone the troops are split up, and enter the departure trenches in small groups. Progress becomes more difficult at every step, for the much-trodden trench is getting sticky. If any rain has fallen the ground becomes a quagmire into which men sink up to their knees at every step. And then, despite instructions, runners, fatigue details, wounded, stretcher-bearers, isolated and lost, block the passage, already cluttered up with abandoned packs, caved-in walls and pitiful corpses. Every crossing is subjected to enemy artillery fire, either in intermittent gusts, killing by surprise, or by a sustained bombardment which stops all movement.

By this time the infantry has reached its starting-point. The men have taken up the positions from which they will shortly launch the assault. Each man checks his arms, wipes the mud off his rifle, stows away his trenching-tool, examines his hand-grenades and divides up his rations. The scaling-ladders are placed against the side of the trench and the machine-guns sited. The officers say a few encouraging words and check their roll.

So long as these material preoccupations remain, nerves are easily dominated. But then comes the wait for zero hour. The wags try a few forced jokes. Wise men try to snatch an hour's sleep. The majority remain silent, absorbed in themselves. Day breaks and anxiety increases. The men know that many of them will never see another dawn. They are tired and shiver in the morning mist. Then, gradually, their torpor disappears with the growing light. Protected by the bombardment and stimulated by the noise and by their own excitement, the infantry risk a glance over the parapet. Anxiously they try to estimate the effectiveness of their artillery fire, for every well-placed shell increases their chances of survival.

The hour of attack is near. Nerves are strained to breaking-point. Watches come out of pockets at every moment. The officers feel that all eyes are upon them. Forcing themselves to remain calm, they make their way along the line, indicating the objective and explaining how to get there. Every man is in the grip of the bonds of discipline.

A few more minutes to go. The men are on their feet. The artillery fire redoubles in intensity. The machine-guns open up to cover the first rush. Zero hour. The officers give the signal. Behind them, with parched throats and throbbing temples, the soldiers go over the top like part of a well-regulated machine.

The attack has been minutely prepared in advance. Every detail concerning the objective, the timing, the troop formations, artillery action and mutual support has been laid down. Nevertheless, almost as soon as it has begun, the carefully organized movement is disrupted by a multitude of causes. The ground is pitted with shell-holes, strewn with wreckage, criss-crossed with trenches and bristling with defensive obstacles of all kinds. The enemy artillery barrage grows from a few intermittent shots to a well-placed deluge of fire. Resistance is weak here, strong there. Sometimes it has been crushed in advance by the artillery preparation, so that the troops occupy their objectives without striking a blow. Sometimes, on the other hand, the infantry comes up against intact firing-points from the very first moment. In most cases, small formations make rapid progress through gaps where the defenders, having been badly cut up, are easily overrun, whilst others are held up by unscathed flanking positions. In any case, the unforeseen eventualities of battle—success to be exploited here, setbacks to be repaired there—demand the intervention of the commander. Reserves have to be brought up and the artillery engaged.

For this purpose a detailed system of liaisons has been elaborated. Field-glasses scour the ground from the observation-points. 'Planes and balloons watch from above. Detachments of artillerymen go forward with the infantry, so as to be able to keep their batteries informed of what is happening. The infantry, for its part, endeavours to send back information by telephone, signals and relays of runners. A complete network of intercommunications joins up commanders' posts, observation-points and intelligence centres. Every department has its maps and plans upon which the information received is plotted. And yet, despite every precaution, communications remain precarious. The O.P.s cannot cover the whole ground, while in the chaos of the attack a thousand details escape their notice. 'Planes and observation balloons are subjected to enemy action. Rain, fog and smoke hamper observation to a greater or lesser degree. Telephone wires are cut, runners killed or wounded. Signals are missed. Allowances have to be made for the unexpected, for delays and mistakes.

It is therefore impossible for the Commander to keep his information up to date or to make decisions in the light of the situation prevailing at the moment. Reserves arrive too late, or else lose their way. Concentrations of artillery-fire miss their target. The troops are a prey to hesitation and doubt. Small units which, by luck or daring, have pushed on far ahead, now find themselves in a perilous position. After suffering heavy losses from counter-attacks, they must either withdraw or be captured. Elsewhere small groups cling on tenaciously. The battle is split up into a series of local actions; the infantry loses its officers and its best men, tactical contact is lost, and the Commander loses control of the operation.

Night brings the welcome opportunity for counting effectives, for reducing the captured ground to some sort of order, for renewing contact with the front, the rear and with both flanks, for moving artillery, replenishing supplies of munitions, food and water and for evacuating wounded and prisoners. The enemy, too, uses the respite for putting his own defences in order. When the second day dawns the attacker is no longer in a position to throw in the same forces as on the previous day. He needs time; time to re-form his exhausted infantry, to reorganize his system of fire, re-establish communications and supply all and sundry. If he resigns himself to these preparations, his enemy's strength will have increased in proportion to the delay involved. If, on the other hand, he resumes the attack there and then, he runs the risk of a costly reverse. Such was the dramatic dilemma which overshadowed every offensive operation of the war.

For, however stringent one's security precautions, it is impossible to keep so many preparations for the attack from the enemy's knowledge. A score of details rouse the vigilance of the defenders; reports from agents, new lines of communication, batteries and trenches revealed by aerial photography; trains, trucks, and troop movements spotted by observers; signs of unusual activity noticed in the front line by units in contact. Raiding parties have brought in prisoners whose interrogation completes the available information.

In the days preceding the battle there is feverish activity; the forward troops, having received reinforcements, improve their positions; the artillery sites its batteries and lays in stocks of ammunition; the engineers repair roads, intercommunications and observation-posts; the air force keeps watch on the enemy. Meanwhile the Commander gives his officers detailed instructions of the tasks which they have to perform, decides how his reserves are to be used and provides everybody with the requisite material.

Suddenly the enemy artillery, which, so far, has been ominously silent, begins its bombardment. First of all it sends over a few isolated shells to get the range. Soon the fire becomes heavier. Guns of every calibre blaze away all at the same time. The deluge of projectiles covers the whole area, leaving no person or place a moment's peace or respite. Stunned and dazed by the deafening barrage, the infantry goes to ground. Heavy shells are crashing into crowded dug-outs. The living and the dead lie inextricably mixed in the shattered trenches. Men are cut off from each other by dust and smoke. All communication between them is made impossible by the din. Leaderless and helpless, suspended between life and death, the troops can do nothing but wait passively for the annihilating blow.

One thing alone might bring some comfort to the stricken infantry—their own artillery. But its voice remains silent, for, subjected to the same pitiless barrage, choked and blinded by the poisonous fumes, the gunners cannot get near their guns. Enemy 'planes fly over the emplacements, and any gun that opens fire is spotted and put out of action. The deluge of shells, which tears up the roads and blocks them with shattered vehicles, blasted trees and dead horses, makes all movement along them impossible. Depots and casualty clearing-stations are unapproachable. No trains can use the railheads in the sector. Working-parties and guards are incapable of carrying out their orders.

The Commander finds himself cut off from his troops, without news or means of action. With telephone wires broken, signals impossible, runners hopelessly lost, he can receive neither reports nor orders. Pounded by high-explosive and blinded by smoke-bombs, observation-posts are useless, while any 'plane or observation-balloon is shot out of the air by swarms of enemy fighters.

For hours, sometimes for days, the artillery barrage pounds positions and breaks spirits. The survivors are depressed and apathetic. Without sleep, food or water, feeling themselves abandoned by God and man, the soldiers have one hope—that their ordeal should end quickly, no matter how.

Now the enemy has gone over to the offensive. But thanks to the curtain of fire which has preceded the attack, the defenders become aware of the situation only when the opposing infantry is upon them. Shells are still falling on their trenches, when a shout of "Here they come!" brings the survivors to their feet. A few yards in front of them, through the dust and smoke, the enemy appears. But the men take some time to pull themselves together, to grab their rifles and fire them, to prime and throw their hand-grenades or get their machine-guns firing. What is more, some of the weapons are so covered with earth that they misfire. The commanders have been killed and gun-teams and firing-parties wiped out. Resistance is sometimes overwhelmed by the first wave of the attack before the defenders have been able to organize themselves.

At certain points, however, either because their defences were stronger or because the nature of the ground gave protection against artillery fire, the defenders have had time to put themselves in readiness. The example has been given by a resolute commander who sees that his orders are carried out. They open fire, somewhat scattered at first, but more sustained at every moment. Automatics rattle. The oncoming enemy crumples up. The defence need fear no attack from the front.

But their flanks are in danger. The pivotal garrison are horrified to see that they are outflanked and then cut off. Now the enemy rakes the ground with concentrated machine-gun fire. There is a murderous close-range battle of hand-grenades. The last defences are wiped out by mortar fire. Flame-throwers sear and burn the occupants. The artillery begins to batter them again with a crescendo of fire. One after another men are being killed. Ammunition runs out. The survivors are parched with thirst. Without orders or news, they lose hope at last. The enemy is upon them. Resistance weakens and dies.

But they have done their job, which was to gain time. The Commander has been able to pick up the threads of the battle, to take the most urgent measures and place his immediate reserves. Reinforcements, taken from neighbouring sectors, have begun to arrive. The artillery, which has now a little information to work on, puts down a heavy barrage, giving new life to the flagging spirits of the troops. The aviation makes good use of the tiredness of the enemy squadrons to risk some reconnaissance flights. Observation-points begin to function again. The network of communications has been restored. Behind the lines, every man gets back to his interrupted job. Convoys are reformed. It becomes possible once more to send up supplies and to evacuate the wounded. Discipline and good order return. In no time a subtle wave of confidence spreads throughout the army. The word goes round: "They won't get through!"

Pitiless, monotonous, and ruinous for defence and attack, such was the war of attrition; huge armies of brave men locked in deadly combat, prodigies of courage, action and skill on both sides; gigantic undertakings completed, destroyed and rebuilt; battles lasting several months, fought on a narrow front with tremendous wastage of life and material; ten million casualties in France alone; a thousand million shells fired. Despite all, the front remained obstinately motionless. No offensive brought a decision, no sacrifices brought victory. The task remained undiminished, and its end as far off as ever. Hope was a matter of faith.

III

For a struggle of this kind France was prepared neither morally nor materially. She had been assured by her economists, her politicians and her soldiers that the war would be short. Nor would the High Command resign itself to the stabilization of the front. The fact that French territory was invaded made patience impossible—"The Germans are still in Noyon." And finally, we had to keep the main part of the enemy's forces on our front in order to save our Russian and Serbian allies and to encourage Italy, Rumania, and Greece to enter the war on our side. The result was that no sooner had the long front line been established before a series of bloody assaults was launched against the enemy's positions. For two years the Allies attacked incessantly without the necessary material.

Nor was this material immediately forthcoming. When, on September 20, 1914, the Minister of War, Millerand, met the leaders of the metallurigcal industry in Bordeaux and called upon them to go all out in the production of vast quantities of munitions, supplies of shells amounted to 900,000 and the State arsenals were turning out only 8,000 a day. A year later, in the offensives in Champagne and Artois, a million 75 mm. shells were fired—that is, thirty per yard of front. In 1916, on the Somme, three times as many were used. But the 75 mm. gun was not adequate for every purpose. Not only were large areas of ground out of its effective range, but it was not powerful enough to destroy well-protected positions. Large numbers of hastily manufactured shells burst prematurely, putting more than six hundred guns out of action in six months. Every type of heavy gun that could be raised from arsenals, forts, or coastal batteries was brought up to the front: 80, 90 and 120 mm. long-barrel Bange pieces, 95 mm. Lahitolles, 120 mm. short-barrel Baquets, antiquated mortars of 220 and 270 mm. calibre. But this out-of-date artillery had neither the necessary range nor rate of fire and the shells were of poor quality. Some of the naval guns, however, proved quite useful weapons. Although the High Command decided in 1915 to demand the manufacture of modern artillery, the guns were not ready for service until the beginning of 1917. Meanwhile the French launched a series of useless and sometimes criminally foolish attacks which resulted in fearful loss of life. In 1915 they lost in France alone 1,350,000 men killed, wounded, and prisoners as against German losses of 550,000 men.

France, with her low birth-rate, paid in human lives for her mistakes and her lack of preparedness, and made a greater blood-sacrifice than any other belligerent. She had more men under arms, in proportion to population, than any other country. At the outset, 3,780,000 men were mobilised, 1,900,000 as front-line troops. Their losses in killed, wounded, and prisoners amounted in 1914 to 955,000 men; in 1915, 1,430,000; in 1916, 900,000; in 1917, 546,000 and in 1918, 1,095,000, making a total of close on 5,000,000. This despite the ever-growing needs of munitions and agriculture which absorbed 1,500,000 servicemen, without counting the others. Yet from the end of 1915 France found the means of bringing the number of front-line troops to the total of 3,000,000 and of maintaining the numbers at that level. To do this it was necessary to call up six new classes, to use over-aged troops in the fighting line, to send men back to the front almost before their wounds were healed, to throw in every man capable of serving, and progressively to lower the physical standard required for recruits. By the end of the war, without counting her native troops, France had incorporated 7,800,000 men, or 20 per cent of the population, in the armed forces. No other nation had done so much. The respective percentages for other countries are: Germany, 18; Italy, 15; Austria-Hungary, 14; Britain, 13; Russia, 10. The number of French soldiers killed amounted to 3.5 per cent of the total population; for Germany the percentage was 2.9; for Britain, 2.2; for Italy, 1.7; for Austria, 0.9; for Russia, 0.7. The sacrifice was especially cruel for France, since it was paid with the lives of her youth, a treasure in which she was poorer than any other European country.

It may seem incredible that a slaughter on such a scale did not have as its consequences the disintegration of the army. Every single French division was engaged on the average ten times. Some of them took part in as many as seventeen actions, without counting long periods during which they occupied a sector. It was an almost invariable rule that no division was relieved until it had lost a third of its effectives. When one considers that the infantry alone suffered more than three-quarters of the total losses, an idea can be formed of the punishment taken by some of its regiments. Certain of them which, thanks to their high quality, had to bear the brunt, incorporated as many as twelve times their normal complement of men. The 19th Battalion of Chasseurs, with an average establishment of 800 men, held the grim and glorious record of losing 12,570 officers, n.c.o.s and men, 3,133 of whom were killed.

As a consequence of these tremendous losses the troops consisted of a heterogeneous collection of men of all ages and origins. Entirely new infantry divisions had to be formed. As against 64 infantry divisions at the beginning of the war, the number rose to 110, while the numbers of the general reserves were multiplied five times. The constantly decimated cadres were unable to cope with these fluctuating masses of new entrants. By the end of 1915 50 per cent of the regular officers had been killed or incapacitated. As time went on, platoons, companies, and even battalions were commanded by officers of the reserve, many of whom learned the art of commanding men, while others never acquired the necessary degree of authority. Almost all of them, unless they were killed or discharged unfit, went through the normal gamut several times—"over the top", hospital, base, and back to the front to reinforce a different corps—so that they never had the time to make that personal contact with their own men which is essential if there is to be cohesion. In this continual reshuffling there could be none of that moving ceremonial which formerly gave a soul to a regiment; no flags were unfurled, no trumpets blared, no forests of bayonets glinted in the sun. Everywhere and always, nothing but mud, dug-outs, and packs.

Yet belief in victory remained long undimmed among the rank and file. "We'll get 'em!" they said. If success had not materialized, it was because they lacked some particular weapon with which they would soon be provided. And they prepared to make yet another effort, which they hoped would be the last.

Yet months and years passed. Resignation gradually gave way under the long anguish of ever-threatening death and unrelieved misery. Then the burden was not fairly distributed, and the soldier became irritated at the differences. He groused or joked about members of the General Staff or others whose duties kept them well behind the front line. A certain unhealthy atmosphere of profiteering, cynicism and excess among the civilians made him more envious of those who could enjoy the things of which he was deprived—comfort, freedom, women. Even the fatuous optimism displayed in the newspapers and in official speeches added to his depression.

Little by little discontent degenerated into lack of discipline. Cases of serious crime punished by courts-martial rose from 3,000 in 1914 to 14,000 in 1915, 25,000 in 1916, reaching the figure of 26,000 for the first four months of 1917. There were many signs—the tone of conversation and letters, the shouts and songs of men on leave, the disorderly conduct of men in camp, the increase in drunkenness—which showed that morale was cracking. The despondency caused by the failure of the April offensive on the Chemin des Dames gave rise to a widespread crisis. During the months of May, June, and July 1917, a large number of units refused to obey orders. In some cases the mutiny was restricted to a kind of sit-down strike: "We're not doing any more attacking", "We're not going into the line again". But in many instances there were open demonstrations. Some indulged in armed rebellion and prepared to march on Paris. In 10 weeks mutinies of this kind affected units in 80 infantry regiments, 21 battalions of chasseurs, and 9 artillery regiments. The mutinous troops belonged to 54 different divisions.

The disease was simply a symptom of overstrain. Pétain did not content himself with repression alone. He endeavoured to find a remedy for the ills which beset the soldier. He lengthened his periods of rest, increased his pay, provided more straw in his quarters. To foster his self-respect he invented stripes and shoulder-cords and made a fairer distribution of medals and citations which, formerly, had been given in inverse proportion to the danger incurred. He strove to bring officers into closer contact with their troops, and encouraged the private soldier to give his opinion. He made a point of explaining the why and wherefore of the decisions which had to be made. In short, the treatment consisted in rest and restoration. For a whole year the only battles fought consisted in three minor offensives which were called off as soon as the first onslaught had gained its objective. The front became a workshop in which the army was forged anew.

For one thing, it had to absorb the equipment produced by an industrial machine which was now working to capacity. The increase in the numbers of machine-guns and the adoption of the automatic rifle brought about the re-organization of the infantry in small gun teams instead of in rifle sections. The artillery, too, had to be transformed in the light of its new material. Each division and each army corps received 24 heavy guns. Batteries of every calibre, 75 and 105 mm. lorry-borne guns, 155, 220 and 270 mm. motor-drawn guns, and 240, 305, 370, and 400 mm. pieces transported by rail formed a mobile reserve which made it possible for the commander to concentrate an enormous weight of fire-power wherever it was needed. The cavalry provided cadres for the infantry as well as contingents of foot-soldiers. Regiments of Schneider, Saint-Chamond, and Renault tanks were constituted to operate in massed formation, thus marking the beginning of the revolution in warfare brought about by the combination of the petrol motor and armour. After a long succession of disappointments the air force now had some excellent machines—Moranes, Spads, and Potez for reconnaissance; Spads and Salmsons as fighters; Bréguets, Voisins, and Farmans as bombers; Nieuports, Letord-Lorraines for home defence—with a total power forty times greater than at the beginning of the war. Numerous schools, centres, and training establishments instructed the troops in the use of their new weapons. After the fourth war winter the army had found its feet again.

In a war of material moral is a consequence of the value of one's equipment, and in this all-important sphere France had succeeded in making good her handicap. Although her pre-war plans envisaged the use of only the number of guns already in existence at the time of the mobilization, 36,000 new cannon were manufactured. In place of the calculated daily production of 14,000 shells, the total actually manufactured was 300,000 a day, and 400 tons of gunpowder instead of the 24 tons which had previously been judged sufficient. During the first fortnight of the Battle of the Somme 3,000 kilos of projectiles were fired for every metre of ground in the fighting zone, while in seven days at La Malmaison the weight of shells fired exceeded 6,000 kilos. As compared with 3,000 automatics in service at the beginning of the war, the total number put into use was in the neighbourhood of 300,000; telephones increased from 2,000 to 35,000; batteries from 2,000 to 3,000,000; cables from 600 to 2,000,000 kilometres; wireless sets from 50 to 30,000 with 300,000 accumulators At the time of the armistice the French army had several thousands of continuous wave radio sets in use, while the Germans were still in the experimental stage with theirs. Whereas on August 2, 1914, the French had 136 aeroplanes with 500 spare engines, 35,000 machines and 180,000 engines were produced during the war. They invented the tank, and 5,000 models were manufactured. Although taken by surprise by the illegal use of poison gas, the French were able to make no mean reply with the new weapon. In addition, they equipped themselves lavishly with field-glasses, range-finders, automatic sights and sound-detectors. Wearing steel helmets and grey-blue or khaki uniforms, well equipped and well fed, the troops at last shook off the irritation and depression caused by the authorities' neglect of detail.

These results are all the more deserving of praise seeing that the invasion of Northern and Eastern France had cost the country 50 per cent of the coal, 64 per cent of the iron, and 62 per cent of the steel normally produced in her mines and works. In addition to these large quantities of fuel and iron, France entirely lacked the copper, zinc and manganese indispensable for the manufacture of munitions. She had none of the cotton or nitrates needed for the production of explosives, nor enough petrol, wool, oil, leather or chemical products. It is true that thanks to her alliance with Britain she was able to import all these raw materials, but they had to be paid for, and the means of obtaining the necessary credits for financing these transactions had to be discovered as and when the need arose.

Moreover, despite the lack of so many necessities, and despite the invasion of her soil, France struck mighty blows outside her own territory. As early as 1915 she had provided two-thirds of the Allied forces landed on Gallipoli. The Balkan expedition was undertaken on French initiative. In September 1918 there were nine French divisions in action on the Vardar. British, Serbian, Italian and Greek troops were under the command of General Franchet d'Espérey, who led them to victory at a pace that was achieved nowhere else. Between Caporetto and the end of the campaign France lent the Italians 40,000 men and powerful forces of artillery. For more than a year the French navy kept the Austrian fleet bottled up in the Adriatic and played an important part in the attempt to force the Dardanelles. French cruisers, torpedo-boats, trawlers and minelayers subsequently accounted for over one-third of the number of German submarines sent to the bottom. In the meantime France had maintained order in her Empire, kept watch on Morocco, expelled the Senussi from Southern Tunisia, and conquered the Congo and the Cameroons. She helped by land and sea to safeguard the Suez Canal, to conquer Jerusalem from the Turks, to liberate Arabia, Syria, the Lebanon, and Cilicia. The Belgian forces were armed entirely by the French, who also received the Serbian army and kept it equipped until the end of the war, expelled King Constantine from Athens and provided the Venezelist troops with arms and equipment. The Rumanians, distant though they were, received French advisers and specialists. In 1916 and 1917 a French military mission sent munitions and supplies to the Russians through Archangel and Kola. The American troops were trained by French instructors; they used French artillery and flew French 'planes. At the time of the armistice a Polish army and a Czechoslovak corps, armed and organized by the French, had recently gone into action on the Western Front. In every corner of the world French prestige and power roused and galvanized the war effort.

But to sustain this prestige and to make use of this power France needed, and found, leaders. It is true that the political game made leadership unstable and stormy. In the space of four years five Premiers formed seven cabinets, while seven different men held office as Minister of War. But while Viviani, Briand, Ribot and Painlevé all pulled in different directions, Poincaré, as head of the State, assured continuity in the country's plans. Steadfast in his aim and firmly seated in the saddle, familiar with every problem and every part of the machine, he was both leader and counsellor. Though his caution led him to disapprove of the war, he saw its approach with a kind of secret hope and toiled ceaselessly to keep his country bent upon her traditional task.

If Poincaré was the wisdom of France, Clemenceau was her anger. Not until the eleventh hour did France call upon this fierce warrior. He was equal to the worst catastrophes. "War—nothing but war!" How well it suited him! He hurled himself upon traitors, whether actual or potential, upon Germany and the House of Austria and rent them tooth and nail. He struck passionately, sometimes blindly—and France paid for his excesses. But, at the time, this impulsive, fierce old man gave her the ruthless tenacity which she needed for her final struggle.

The military side too was now well in hand. The distinguished leaders who had borne the burden during the experimental stage—Dubail, Castelnau, Ruffey, Langle de Cary, Lanrezac, Maunoury, d'Amade—were gradually joined or replaced by men like Franchet d'Espérey, Sarrail, Fayolle, Guillaumat, Nivelle, Maistre, Gouraud, Mangin, Humbert, Debeney, Degoutte, past-masters in the harsh tactics of cannon *versus* well protected machine-guns. The generals were supported by staff officers experienced in every table and every computation designed to aid the judgment in using the enormous mass of material to best advantage. Most important of all, there had emerged a leader who taught his army to distinguish the real from the imaginary and the possible from the impossible. On the day when a choice had to be made between ruin and reason, Pétain received promotion. With an unerring flair for essentials and practicabilities, not only did he dominate his task by the power of his intellect, but he impressed upon it the mark of his character. This clear-minded personality seemed appointed by Nature to provide that sober judgment in action which the struggle and its participants demanded. A man who had disdained to climb by the favour of others inspired confidence in his subordinates. His acute critical sense had preserved him from easy success. His independence and integrity, while allowing him to take orders and receive advice, made him immune from influence. His studied reserve of manner, accompanied by an observant irony and a proud dignity, preserved the secret of his power from the gaze of the multitude.

Yet tactics which consisted in an alternation of methodical attack with well-conceived defence, though gaining successes, were unable to bring victory. Victory could be achieved only by a combination of a number of all-out efforts. What was needed was a synthesis of every separate operation in one, an obstinate readiness to double the stakes and to take risks—these are the essentials of strategy.

When Foch arrived, Fate dealt him a handful of trumps. It is difficult to see what his daring planning could have achieved had it not been for Pétain's well-constructed machine, Haig's army and Pershing's effectives. Nevertheless, to Foch belongs the honour of having imposed his will, the merit of playing the last high stakes, the glory of seeing the business through, if not to triumph, at least to victory. He was, moreover, an accomplished strategist, and not one of the lines and arrows on his map of operations lends itself to criticism.

As soon as the situation had been restored, he began a cautious offensive, restricted at first to a limited operation in the neighbourhood of Villers-Cotterets. Soon the offensive reached the Ancre, then the Somme, moving towards Saint-Mihiel. Once this movement was under way it spread to wider sectors of the front. One after another, Picardy, Champagne, the Argonne and Flanders, all became involved in it. The whole front was on the move, from Verdun to the North Sea. As the enemy gave way, our hammer-blows struck harder and faster. In this battle which, in three months, forced the enemy to capitulate, the French army gave undisputed proof of its superiority. During the months of August, September, and October 1918 the French fired an average of 600,000 shells a day, and the Germans 500,000, a third of which were directed against France's allies. The French had 3,000 'planes in the air against 2,600 of the enemy's. The attack was supported by 3,000 tanks while the Germans possessed less than 60. We had 80,000 lorries as compared with 40,000 at most on the other side. As for the skill displayed by the High Command, the General Staff and the Services, and the quality of the troops, the results speak for themselves. Without respite or setback they captured every position in which the enemy attempted to make a stand. Though opposed almost to the last day by divisions equal in number to their own, in twelve weeks the French killed or wounded more than 500,000 Germans, took 140,000 prisoners, and captured 5,000 guns and 28,000 machine-guns, for the loss of 260,000 men. When the Germans begged for an armistice, Castelnau was about to launch from Lorraine an attack on the enemy's communications which would have cornered his armies in some gigantic Sedan.

Although caught unprepared for the first onslaught, France had recovered herself on the very edge of the abyss. Still staggering from her wounds she had plunged into a gruelling series of battles, from which, armed at last for victory, she emerged victorious. She had paid dearly for her omissions in preparing for the struggle. Numerically inferior for the first time in history, she had lost the advantage enjoyed by the big battalions. Yet among the armies united against the Central Powers, her army played the leading part from the beginning to the end. More cruelly tried by the suffering of war and invasion than any other nation, by the sacrifice of the best of her sons, by the grievous wounds inflicted on her soil, by devastated homes and shattered families, she had forged for herself a fighting machine which finally surpassed that of any other belligerent. In the final reckoning, two out of every three Germans killed met their death at the hands of French soldiers. French guns, 'planes, and tanks were second to none. French generalship showed itself to be unsurpassed. The victorious powers drew inspiration from the undaunted effort of French valour.

Throughout the centuries the French people have enjoyed the sad privilege of bearing with unflinching courage the heaviest load of sorrows. If neither age nor experience has rid this people of its shortcomings, disaster has been unavailing against its inextinguishable vitality and faith in its destiny. Though at times forgetful of its strength in the pursuit of phantoms, it has shown itself invincible once it has turned its back upon them. A great people, fit to show others the way, fit for enterprise and combat, for ever playing the leading role in the drama of history, whether as tyrant, as victim, or as champion of the oppressed; a people whose genius, whether in eclipse or in glory, has always found its faithful reflection in the mirror of its army.

THE END